celebrating
ICE CREAM
AND CAKE

By

Avner Laskin

A LEISURE ARTS PUBLICATION

Vice President and Chief Operations Officer: Tom Siebenmorgen
Vice President, Sales and Marketing: Pam Stebbins
Vice President, Operations: Jim Dittrich
Editor in Chief: Susan White Sullivan
Director of Designer Relations: Debra Nettles
Senior Art Director: Rhonda Shelby
Senior Prepress Director: Mark Hawkins

Produced for Leisure Arts, Inc. by Penn Publishing Ltd.
www.penn.co.il
Editor: Rachel Wagner
Culinary editing: Tamar Zakut
Design and layout: Ariane Rybski
Photography: Daniel Lailah
Food styling: Amit Farber
Special thanks to "Hafatzim" www.hafatzim.com

PRINTED IN CHINA

ISBN-13: 978-1-60900-011-0
Library of Congress Control Number: 2009940701

Cover photography by Daniel Lailah

Contents

Introduction • 4

Ice Cream Basics • 6

Ice Cream Toppings and Sauces • 38

Sorbets • 56

Ice Cream Desserts • 72

Ice Cream Cakes • 92

Cakes for Special Occasions • 114

Tools and Ingredients • 140

Metric Equivalents • 142

Index • 144

Introduction

At our house ice cream isn't a seasonal affair. I'm an ice cream lover in summer and winter alike, as is the rest of my family. Making your own ice cream is a truly exciting and magical process. Basic ingredients like cream, sugar and eggs enter the ice cream maker and a short while later are transformed into ice cream! This transformation from liquid to fresh airy ice cream is a thrilling process that never ceases to awe kids and adults alike. Not only is making the ice cream a fun family activity, but eating it turns into a wonderful community affair, with the kids inviting their friends over to enjoy the spoils.

When it comes to birthdays, holidays, special occasions or even elegant dinner parties, we always start the planning with what's for dessert. Following a series of simple steps can make stunning, stylish cakes at home – you'll be sure to awe your guests with a store-bought look and full homemade flavor.

There are many other advantages to making ice cream, cakes and desserts at home. First of all, you know exactly which ingredients are going into it, so there isn't any concern about artificial flavors, colors or preservatives. When it comes to ice cream, you can also suit it to the personal preferences of your family and friends: soft ice cream for those who like it smooth, hard ice cream for those who prefer it chunky, and anything and everything in between.

The easiest way to make ice cream at home is with the use of an ice cream maker. As you get to know your ice cream maker, you'll better understand how long it takes to achieve your desired consistency. All the ice creams in this book have been made in my home kitchen with the second type of ice cream maker mentioned below (see *Equipment Notes*, page 8).

Festive dessert making at home is just plain fun. You can get your children involved and there is unlimited room for creativity. In **Celebrating Ice Cream and Cake** you will first learn to make basic recipes for ice creams, sorbets, cakes and mousse cakes. Once you've got your bases covered, you'll be free to expand with ideas from the rest of the book – or to let your imaginations run wild. Just pay attention to the main principles outlined and enjoy!

About the Author

Ice cream aficionado Avner Laskin studied at the prestigious "Cordon Bleu Academy" in Paris, where he received the "Grand Diplôme de Cuisine and Pâtisserie". He later specialized in traditional breads under the world-renowned Jean-Louis Clément at the "Lenôtre School", also in Paris, and was awarded the coveted "Diplôme de Pain de Tradition et de Qualité" in 1998. Laskin's culinary career includes internships at two-star Michelin restaurants in France and Germany, and extensive work as a restaurant consultant—specializing in kitchen design and recipe and menu development. He is the author of several cookbooks.

Ice Cream Basics

The Golden Rules of Ice Cream

·

Italian Vanilla Ice Cream

·

French Vanilla Ice Cream

·

Egg-less Vanilla Ice Cream

·

Apricot Ape Ice Cream

·

Berry Vanilla Bramble Ice Cream

·

Blueberry Vanilla Nights Ice Cream

·

Strawberry-licious Vanilla Ice Cream

·

Pleasing Pistachio Ice Cream

·

Mediterranean Marzipan Ice Cream

·

Jackie D. Chocolate Ice Cream

·

Coffee-Biscuit Break Ice Cream

·

Pure Passion Ice Cream

·

Tropical Treat Ice Cream

·

Candied Pecan and Peanut Butter Explosion Ice Cream

·

Chocolate Fudge Thud Ice Cream

·

Chocolate Brownie Bump Ice Cream

·

Candied Fruit Freak Ice Cream

The Golden Rules of Ice Cream

Before you begin making your own ice cream, please read the following. You should also plan and review the recipe thoroughly in advance to ensure that both making and eating the ice cream will be a fun experience.

Equipment Notes

The Ice Cream Maker:

• There are 3 types of home ice cream makers on the market.

   • The first and simplest one doesn't have a cooler. In this case, you need to chill the ice cream mixture almost to the point of freezing, then place the entire ice cream maker in the freezer where it will mix and freeze the ice cream.

   • The second ice cream maker has a cooler and a double-walled pot, in which you place the mixture. The ice cream maker chills while it mixes so that as the ice cream is cooling, air is added. This results in a light consistency.

   • The third ice cream maker is a low-volume industrial machine. This ice cream maker works in a similar way to the previous two, but the cooling output is different. This ice cream maker turns the liquid mixture into ice cream in a matter of minutes and can absorb a lot of air, creating an especially light ice cream.

• Thoroughly clean the bowl in your ice cream maker in hot soapy water before each use (unless the ice cream maker instructions say otherwise).

Ingredient Notes

• Always use the freshest and highest quality ingredients when making your ice cream. The quality of the ingredients determines the quality of the ice cream. The fresher and tastier the ingredients, the tastier your ice cream will be.

• Always use fresh milk and fresh large eggs. When milk is called for, use whole milk with at least 3% fat content.

• There are many different types of vanilla flavoring. The best type for making ice cream is pure vanilla liquid extract or a vanilla bean. One teaspoon of vanilla extract is equivalent to half a vanilla bean.

• When using a vanilla bean, slit the bean in half lengthwise and cook the halved bean with the other ingredients, as instructed. At the end of the cooking process, remove the bean and scrape vanilla residue back into the cooked mixture.

- You can substitute white sugar with brown sugar.

- You may also substitute the sugar with any other type of sweetener.

- If you choose to substitute, remember that each sweetener has a different level of sweetness, mass, and texture. Therefore, mastering sugar substitution is a learning process.

- In recipes that call for chocolate, always use the highest quality bittersweet chocolate, containing at least 55% cocoa.

- In recipes that call for fruit, use ripe, but not over-ripe fruit.

- You can use frozen fruit, but it must be thoroughly defrosted before use.

Process Notes

- For egg-based ice creams, you must use a thermometer (see *Candy Thermometer*, page 140) during cooking. The desired temperature must be reached. Any deviation from the requested temperature will alter the consistency of the eggs and affect the success of the final product. (For example, if the temperature is too high, the eggs will scramble.)

- The cooked liquid mixture should be refrigerated for a minimum of 4 hours, but no more than 48 hours. When possible, I recommend preparing the mixture a day in advance and refrigerating it overnight. This enables the flavors to meld better and leaves less work for the ice cream maker.

- When you pour the mixture into the ice maker, be sure not to fill it more than two-thirds. The contents expand as they freeze.

- The ice cream consistency is determined by the amount of time it is mixed in the ice cream maker. The times vary from machine to machine. The general rule of thumb is: the longer you mix the ice cream in the ice cream maker, the harder and denser it will be. The consistency and lightness of the ice cream is a matter of personal taste. Therefore, in most recipes we let you decide on the mixing time.

- Taste the ice cream while mixing until you get to know your ice cream maker and discover how long it takes to achieve your preferred consistency.

• You may substitute any of the liquids in the recipes, as long as the amounts and ratios are the same as in the recipe. For example, you can make ice cream using only cream. Alternately, you can substitute with whole milk, using no cream at all. You can also substitute with yogurt, as long as it's the liquid type meant for drinking.

• You can also use coconut, rice, almond or soy milk as liquid substitutes for cream or milk. Just pay attention to the amount of sugar in the recipe if the liquids are sweetened. It's important to first taste the substitute you choose, as some of them have their own distinct flavors which will be discernable in the ice cream.

• For chocolate ice cream: To ensure a smooth, non-grainy texture, mix the melted liquid chocolate in with the ice cream base when it's still hot from cooking.

• For recipes that include alcohol: to ensure the best alcohol or liqueur taste, mix the alcohol in with the ice cream while the ice cream base is still hot from cooking. You may increase or reduce the amount of alcohol to your taste. Just keep in mind that the more alcohol in the ice cream, the longer it will take to freeze. You may also choose to eliminate the alcohol entirely from any of the recipes.

• Once the ice cream is ready, don't store it for more than three or four days because it's likely to develop an aftertaste.

Italian Vanilla Ice Cream

Makes
10
scoops

This airy ice cream makes the ideal base for a wide range of flavors. The base is very sweet so there is no need to add additional sugar if you mix in another flavor. Store as a base for up to two days in the refrigerator.

INGREDIENTS

1 cup milk

1 cup whipping cream

1 teaspoon pure vanilla extract

¾ cup sugar

4 egg yolks

Store as an ice cream for up to five days in the freezer

PREPARATION

1. Place milk, cream, vanilla, and half the sugar in a saucepan and bring to a boil over medium heat.

2. Place egg yolks and the remaining sugar into a bowl and whisk together by hand until smooth and fully combined.

3. When the saucepan contents come to a boil, reduce heat and quickly pour in the egg yolk mixture.

4. Stir contents with a wooden spoon and cook until the temperature reaches 175°F, then remove from heat.

5. Pour the mixture into a clean bowl through a fine sieve in order to achieve a smooth, lump-free consistency.

6. Cover the bowl in plastic cling wrap, allow it to cool slightly, and then place it in the refrigerator for a minimum of 4 hours to ensure a very cold mixture.

7. Pour the mixture into an ice cream maker and run until preferred ice cream consistency is achieved – soft or firm.

French Vanilla Ice Cream

Makes

10

scoops

This is a basic recipe for an ice cream that isn't too sweet. The high proportion of egg yolks enables the prepared ice cream to better hold its creamy structure and can therefore be stored in the freezer for longer.

INGREDIENTS

1½ cups milk

½ cup whipping cream

1 teaspoon pure vanilla extract

⅔ cup sugar

6 egg yolks

Store as a base for up to two days in the refrigerator, or store as an ice cream for up to eight days in the freezer. If you add other flavoring to the recipe, test the level of sweetness before pouring into the ice cream maker.

PREPARATION

1. Place milk, cream, vanilla, and half the sugar in a saucepan and bring to a boil over medium heat.

2. Place egg yolks and the remaining sugar into a bowl and whisk together by hand until smooth and fully combined.

3. When the saucepan contents come to a boil, reduce heat and quickly pour in the egg yolk mixture.

4. Stir contents with a wooden spoon and cook until the temperature reaches 175°F, then remove from heat.

5. Pour the mixture into a clean bowl through a fine sieve in order to achieve a smooth, lump-free consistency.

6. Cover the bowl in plastic cling wrap, allow it to cool slightly, and then place in the refrigerator for at least 4 hours to ensure a very cold mixture.

7. Pour the mixture into an ice cream maker and run until preferred ice cream consistency is achieved – soft or firm.

Egg-less Vanilla Ice Cream

Makes

10

scoops

This egg-free ice cream base is just like the one used in Italian gelaterias and can be made into a variety of flavors.

INGREDIENTS

½ cup milk

1½ cups whipping cream

1 teaspoon pure vanilla extract

¾ cup white sugar

Because of the lack of egg yolks, this ice cream can only be stored in the freezer for up to two days. Due to this recipe's high sugar content, you probably won't have to add any extra sugar if you want to create various flavors from it. This ice cream is about as sweet as the Italian Vanilla Ice Cream (page 11), so you can easily interchange them in the recipes to come.

PREPARATION

1. Place milk, cream, vanilla, and sugar in a saucepan and bring to a boil over medium heat, then transfer to a bowl.

2. Cover the bowl in plastic cling wrap, then allow it to cool on the counter for 30 minutes.

3. Place in the refrigerator for a minimum of 4 hours to ensure a very cold mixture.

4. Pour the mixture into an ice cream maker and run until preferred ice cream consistency is achieved – soft or firm.

Apricot Ape Ice Cream

Makes

12

scoops

This is a wonderfully refreshing flavor for hot summer days. Use very ripe apricots to ensure a high level of sweetness. If you like this flavor, see the Apricot and Cherry Ice Cream Cake recipe on page 99.

INGREDIENTS

1½ cups milk

1 cup whipping cream

1 teaspoon pure vanilla extract

⅔ cup sugar

6 egg yolks

½ pound fresh apricots, coarsely chopped

3 tablespoons sugar (to mix with the fruit)

1 teaspoon lemon juice

I chose to use the French Vanilla Ice Cream (page 12) as a base in this recipe, but you can substitute others. If you choose to use the Italian Vanilla Ice Cream (page 11), reduce the amount of sugar in the recipe by two tablespoons.

PREPARATION

1. Place milk, cream, vanilla, and half the sugar in a saucepan and bring to a boil over medium heat.

2. Place egg yolks and the remaining sugar into a bowl and whisk together by hand until smooth and fully combined.

3. When the saucepan contents come to a boil, reduce heat and quickly pour in the egg yolk mixture.

4. Stir contents with a wooden spoon and cook until the temperature reaches 175°F, then remove from heat.

5. Pour the mixture into a clean bowl through a fine sieve in order to achieve a smooth, lump-free consistency.

6. Cover the bowl in plastic cling wrap and allow it to cool slightly.

7. Place the mixture in the refrigerator for a minimum of 4 hours to ensure a very cold mixture.

8. Place the apricots, sugar and lemon juice in a bowl, stir and set it aside for 2 hours.

9. Take the mixture out of the refrigerator and mix in the apricots.

10. Pour the mixture into an ice cream maker and run until preferred ice cream consistency is achieved – soft or firm.

Berry Vanilla Bramble Ice Cream

Makes

10

scoops

This ice cream has a light, delicate and very unique flavor. If you like this flavor, see the Berry Vanilla Bramble Ice Cream Tart recipe on page 111.

INGREDIENTS

1 cup milk

1 cup whipping cream

1 teaspoon pure vanilla extract

¾ cup sugar

4 egg yolks

½ pound mixed berries, fresh or frozen

I chose to use the Italian Vanilla Ice Cream (page 11) as a base in this recipe, but you can substitute others. If you choose to use the French Vanilla Ice Cream (page 12), add two tablespoons of sugar to the recipe.

PREPARATION

1. Place milk, cream, vanilla, and half the sugar in a saucepan and bring to a boil over medium heat.

2. Place egg yolks and the remaining sugar into a bowl and whisk together by hand until smooth and fully combined.

3. When the saucepan contents come to a boil, reduce heat and quickly pour in the egg yolk mixture.

4. Stir contents with a wooden spoon and cook until the temperature reaches 175°F, then remove from heat.

5. Pour the mixture into a clean bowl through a fine sieve in order to achieve a smooth, lump-free consistency.

6. Cover the bowl in plastic cling wrap, allow it to cool slightly, and then place it in the refrigerator for a minimum of 4 hours to ensure a very cold mixture.

7. In the meantime, if you are using frozen berries defrost them.

8. Pour the mixture into an ice cream maker, add the berries, and run the machine until preferred ice cream consistency is achieved – soft or firm.

Blueberry Vanilla Nights Ice Cream

This is one of the most loved and well-known flavors. Serve it with homemade apple pie for a winning combination.

INGREDIENTS

1½ cups milk

½ cup whipping cream

1 teaspoon pure vanilla extract

¾ cup sugar

4 egg yolks

½ pound blueberries (fresh or frozen)

1 teaspoon lemon juice

I chose to use the Italian Vanilla Ice Cream (page 11) as my base, but you can easily select a different one. If you choose to use the French Vanilla Ice Cream (page 12), add 2 tablespoons of sugar to the recipe.

PREPARATION

1. Place milk, cream, vanilla, and half the sugar in a saucepan and bring to a boil over medium heat.

2. Place egg yolks and the remaining sugar into a bowl and whisk together by hand until smooth and fully combined.

3. When the saucepan contents come to a boil, reduce heat and quickly pour in the egg yolk mixture.

4. Stir contents with a wooden spoon and cook until the temperature reaches 175°F, then remove from heat.

5. Pour the mixture into a clean bowl through a fine sieve in order to achieve a smooth, lump-free consistency.

6. Cover the bowl in plastic cling wrap, allow it to cool slightly, and then place it in the refrigerator for a minimum of 4 hours to ensure a very cold mixture.

7. In the meantime, if you are using frozen berries defrost them.

8. Place blueberries in a bowl with lemon juice and stir together.

9. Take the mixture out of the refrigerator and mix in blueberries.

10. Pour the mixture into an ice cream maker and run until preferred ice cream consistency is achieved – soft or firm.

Strawberry-licious Vanilla Ice Cream

Makes

10

scoops

This is a splendid combination of good vanilla ice cream and strawberries. When I want to spoil myself, I enjoy a scoop of this fabulous ice cream.

INGREDIENTS

1½ cups milk

½ cup whipping cream

1 teaspoon pure vanilla extract

⅔ cup sugar

6 egg yolks

½ pound fresh strawberries

1 teaspoon lemon juice

I chose to use the French Vanilla Ice Cream (page 12) as a base here, but you can also choose a different one. If you choose to use the Italian Vanilla Ice Cream (page 11), reduce the amount of sugar in the recipe by two tablespoons.

PREPARATION

1. Place milk, cream, vanilla, and half the sugar in a saucepan and bring to a boil over medium heat.

2. Place egg yolks and the remaining sugar into a bowl and whisk together by hand until smooth and fully combined.

3. When the saucepan contents come to a boil, reduce heat and quickly pour in the egg yolk mixture.

4. Stir contents with a wooden spoon and cook until the temperature reaches 175°F, then remove from heat.

5. Pour the mixture into a clean bowl through a fine sieve in order to achieve a smooth, lump-free consistency.

6. Cover the bowl in plastic cling wrap, allow it to cool slightly, and then place it in the refrigerator for a minimum of 4 hours to ensure a very cold mixture.

7. Place the strawberries and the lemon juice in another bowl and stir.

8. Take the mixture out of the refrigerator and mix in the strawberries.

9. Pour the mixture into an ice cream maker and run until preferred ice cream consistency is achieved – soft or firm.

Pleasing Pistachio Ice Cream

Makes

12

scoops

This is the flavor most identified with Sicilian ice cream. I chose to use the Italian Vanilla Ice Cream (page 11) as a base in this recipe, but you can substitute others.

INGREDIENTS

1½ cups milk

1 cup whipping cream

1 teaspoon pure vanilla extract

¾ cup sugar

4 egg yolks

1 cup roasted pistachios, finely chopped

If you choose to use the French Vanilla Ice Cream (page 12), add two tablespoons of sugar to this recipe.

PREPARATION

1. Place milk, cream, vanilla, and half the sugar in a saucepan and bring to a boil over medium heat.

2. Place egg yolks and the remaining sugar into a bowl and whisk together by hand until smooth and fully combined.

3. When the saucepan contents come to a boil, reduce heat and quickly pour in the egg yolk mixture.

4. Stir contents with a wooden spoon and cook until the temperature reaches 175°F, then remove from heat.

5. Pour the mixture into a clean bowl through a fine sieve in order to achieve a smooth, lump-free consistency.

6. Cover the bowl in plastic cling wrap, allow it to cool slightly, and then place it in the refrigerator for a minimum of 4 hours to ensure a very cold mixture.

7. Take the mixture out of the refrigerator and mix in the pistachios.

8. Pour the mixture into an ice cream maker and run until preferred ice cream consistency is achieved – soft or firm.

Mediterranean Marzipan Ice Cream

Makes

10

scoops

This ice cream reminds me of the Mediterranean flavors of the south of France. If you like it, see the Grilled Peaches with Amaretto Sauce and Mediterranean Marzipan Ice Cream recipe on page 81.

INGREDIENTS

1 cup milk

1 cup whipping cream

1 teaspoon pure vanilla extract

¾ cup sugar

4 egg yolks

1 tablespoon amaretto liqueur

6 ounces marzipan, broken into crumbs

I chose to use the Italian Vanilla Ice Cream (page 11) as a base in this recipe, but you can substitute others. If you choose to use the French Vanilla Ice Cream (page 12), add two tablespoons of sugar to the recipe.

PREPARATION

1. Place milk, cream, vanilla, and half the sugar in a saucepan and bring to a boil over medium heat.

2. Place egg yolks and the remaining sugar into a bowl and whisk together by hand until smooth and fully combined.

3. When the saucepan contents come to a boil, reduce heat and quickly pour in the egg yolk mixture.

4. Stir contents with a wooden spoon and cook until the temperature reaches 175°F, then remove from heat.

5. Pour the mixture into a clean bowl through a fine sieve in order to achieve a smooth, lump-free consistency. Stir in the amaretto.

6. Cover the bowl in plastic cling wrap, allow it to cool slightly, and then place it in the refrigerator for a minimum of 4 hours to ensure a very cold mixture.

7. Pour the mixture into an ice cream maker, add the marzipan, and run the machine until preferred ice cream consistency is achieved – soft or firm.

Jackie D. Chocolate Ice Cream

Makes

12

scoops

This is the ice cream for big time chocolate lovers. The combination of high quality bittersweet chocolate and Jack Daniels makes this ice cream something very special.

INGREDIENTS

1 cup milk

1½ cups whipping cream

1 teaspoon pure vanilla extract

¾ cup sugar

4 egg yolks

5 ounces bittersweet chocolate, at least 60% cocoa content

2 tablespoons Jack Daniels

I chose to use the Italian Vanilla Ice Cream (page 11) as a base in this recipe, but you can substitute others. If you choose to use the French Vanilla Ice Cream (page 12), add two tablespoons of sugar to the recipe.

PREPARATION

1. Place milk, cream, vanilla, and half the sugar in a saucepan and bring to a boil over medium heat.

2. Place egg yolks and the remaining sugar into a bowl and whisk together by hand until smooth and fully combined.

3. When the saucepan contents come to a boil, reduce heat and quickly pour in the egg yolk mixture.

4. Stir contents with a wooden spoon and cook until the temperature reaches 175°F, then remove from heat.

5. Pour the mixture into a clean bowl through a fine sieve in order to achieve a smooth, lump-free consistency.

6. Melt the chocolate in the microwave. Quickly add the melted chocolate into the mixture and stir.

7. Add the Jack Daniels and stir.

8. Cover the bowl in plastic cling wrap, allow it to cool slightly, and then place it in the refrigerator for a minimum of 4 hours to ensure a very cold mixture.

9. Pour the mixture into an ice cream maker and run until preferred ice cream consistency is achieved – soft or firm.

Coffee-Biscuit Break Ice Cream

Makes

12

scoops

*This is an interpretation of one of Ben and Jerry's most popular flavors—
the one we never get tired of!*

INGREDIENTS

1½ cups milk

1 cup whipping cream

1 teaspoon pure vanilla extract

⅔ cup sugar

6 egg yolks

½ cup quality Italian espresso

1 cup cookie chunks (plain or chocolate)

For decoration

Roasted espresso beans

*I chose to use the French Vanilla
Ice Cream (page 12) as a base in
this recipe, but you can substitute
others. If you choose to use the
Italian Vanilla Ice Cream (page
11), reduce the amount of sugar in
the recipe by two tablespoons.*

PREPARATION

1. Place milk, cream, vanilla, and half the sugar in a saucepan and bring to a boil over medium heat.

2. Place egg yolks and the remaining sugar into a bowl and whisk together by hand until smooth and fully combined.

3. When the saucepan contents come to a boil, reduce heat and quickly pour in the egg yolk mixture.

4. Stir contents with a wooden spoon and cook until the temperature reaches 175°F, then remove from heat.

5. Pour the mixture into a clean bowl through a fine sieve in order to achieve a smooth, lump-free consistency.

6. Cover the bowl in plastic cling wrap and allow it to cool slightly.

7. Add the espresso.

8. Place the mixture in the refrigerator for a minimum of 4 hours to ensure a very cold mixture.

9. Take the mixture out of the refrigerator and mix in the cookie chunks.

10. Pour the mixture into an ice cream maker and run until preferred ice cream consistency is achieved – soft or firm.

11. Top scoops of ice cream with a few roasted espresso beans before serving.

Pure Passion Ice Cream

Makes

12

scoops

This ice cream, rich with a delicate tartness, is a dessert unto itself. Lovers of exotic flavors will fall in love with this unique ice cream.

INGREDIENTS

1½ cups milk

1 cup whipping cream

1 teaspoon pure vanilla extract

⅔ cup sugar

4 egg yolks

½ pound passion fruit purée (you can also use defrosted frozen purée)

I chose to use the Italian Vanilla Ice Cream (page 11) as a base in this recipe, but you can substitute others. If you choose to use the French Vanilla Ice Cream (page 12), add two tablespoons of sugar to the recipe.

PREPARATION

1. Place milk, cream, vanilla, and half the sugar in a saucepan and bring to a boil over medium heat.

2. Place egg yolks and the remaining sugar into a bowl and whisk together by hand until smooth and fully combined.

3. When the saucepan contents come to a boil, reduce heat and quickly pour in the egg yolk mixture.

4. Stir contents with a wooden spoon and cook until the temperature reaches 175°F, then remove from heat.

5. Pour the mixture into a clean bowl through a fine sieve in order to achieve a smooth, lump-free consistency.

6. Cover the bowl in plastic cling wrap, allow it to cool slightly, and then place it in the refrigerator for a minimum of 4 hours to ensure a very cold mixture.

7. Take the mixture out of the refrigerator and mix in the passion fruit purée.

8. Pour the mixture into an ice cream maker and run until preferred ice cream consistency is achieved – soft or firm.

Tropical Treat Ice Cream

Makes

12

scoops

Take one bite of this excellent ice cream and you'll feel like you're on a Carribean island vacation. The combination of tropical fruit with vanilla ice cream creates a varied range of amazing flavors.

INGREDIENTS

1½ cups milk

1 cup whipping cream

1 teaspoon pure vanilla extract

⅔ cup sugar

4 egg yolks

½ cup fresh pineapple, finely chopped

½ cup fresh mango, finely chopped

½ cup lychee, finely chopped

2 tablespoons demerara sugar (to mix with the fruit)

1 tablespoon Cachaça, or dark rum

1 teaspoon lemon juice

I chose to use the Italian Vanilla Ice Cream (page 11) as a base in this recipe, but you can substitute others. If you choose to use the French Vanilla Ice Cream (page 12), add two tablespoons of sugar to the recipe.

PREPARATION

1. Place milk, cream, vanilla, and half the sugar in a saucepan and bring to a boil over medium heat.

2. Place egg yolks and the remaining sugar into a bowl and whisk together by hand until smooth and fully combined.

3. When the saucepan contents come to a boil, reduce heat and quickly pour in the egg yolk mixture.

4. Stir contents with a wooden spoon and cook until the temperature reaches 175°F, then remove from heat.

5. Pour the mixture into a clean bowl through a fine sieve in order to achieve a smooth, lump-free consistency.

6. Cover the bowl in plastic cling wrap, allow it to cool slightly, and then place it in the refrigerator for a minimum of 4 hours to ensure a very cold mixture.

7. Place the pineapple, mango, lychee, demerara sugar, Cachaça and lemon juice in a bowl, stir and set it aside for 2 hours.

8. Take the mixture out of the refrigerator and mix in the fruit mixture.

9. Pour the mixture into an ice cream maker and run until preferred ice cream consistency is achieved – soft or firm.

Candied Pecan and Peanut Butter Explosion Ice Cream

Makes

10

scoops

Perfect for peanut butter lovers, this rich complex flavor is a quality dessert in a class of its own. If you like this flavor, see the Candied Pecan and Peanut Butter Explosion Ice Cream Pie recipe on page 103.

INGREDIENTS

¼ cup sugar (for the pecans)

½ cup pecans, chopped

1 porcelain dinner plate, covered in ½ tablespoon canola oil

1 cup milk

1 cup whipping cream

1 teaspoon pure vanilla extract

⅔ cup sugar

6 egg yolks

⅔ cup peanut butter

Peanuts for garnish

I chose to use the French Vanilla Ice Cream (page 12) as a base in this recipe, but you can substitute others. If you choose to use the Italian Vanilla Ice Cream (page 11), reduce the amount of sugar in the recipe by two tablespoons.

PREPARATION

1. Put a ¼ cup sugar in a saucepan. Stir with a wooden spoon while heating over medium heat until sugar turns golden. Be careful not to let the sugar burn.

2. Add the pecans to the saucepan and continue cooking on low heat until the pecans turn golden brown. Do not stir.

3. Using the wooden spoon, transfer the pecans onto the porcelain plate. Set aside for half an hour.

4. Place milk, cream, vanilla, and half the sugar into a saucepan and bring to a boil over medium heat.

5. Place egg yolks and the remaining sugar into a bowl and whisk together by hand until smooth and fully combined.

6. When the saucepan contents come to a boil, reduce heat and quickly pour in the egg yolk mixture.

7. Stir contents with a wooden spoon and cook until the temperature reaches 175°F, then remove from heat.

8. Pour the mixture into a clean bowl through a fine sieve in order to achieve a smooth, lump-free consistency.

(continued on page 32)

(continued from page 30)

9. Place the candied pecans in a food processor and grind into crumbs, then transfer to the bowl of hot liquid mixture and stir.

10. Cover the bowl in plastic cling wrap, allow it to cool slightly, and then place it in the refrigerator for a minimum of 4 hours to ensure a very cold mixture.

11. Pour the mixture into an ice cream maker and run until a very soft ice cream is achieved.

12. Add half the peanut butter, run the machine for one minute, then stop.

13. Add the rest of the peanut butter and run the machine until preferred ice cream consistency is achieved – soft or firm.

14. Top with peanuts for extra peanut flavor and a satisfying crunch, as seen in the picture.

Chocolate Fudge Thud Ice Cream

Makes

10

scoops

The rich, concentrated chocolate flavor of this ice cream is reserved for true chocolate enthusiasts. If you are one such enthusiast, see the Chocolate Fudge Ice Cream Pie recipe on page 95.

INGREDIENTS

1½ cups milk

½ cup whipping cream

1 teaspoon pure vanilla extract

⅔ cup sugar

6 egg yolks

½ cup whipping cream

5 ounces bittersweet chocolate

I chose to use the French Vanilla Ice Cream (page 12) as a base in this recipe, but you can substitute others. If you choose to use the Italian Vanilla Ice Cream (page 11), reduce the amount of sugar in the recipe by two tablespoons.

PREPARATION

1. Place milk, ½ cup cream, vanilla, and half the sugar in a saucepan and bring to a boil over medium heat.

2. Place egg yolks and the remaining sugar into a bowl and whisk together by hand until smooth and fully combined.

3. When the saucepan contents come to a boil, reduce heat and quickly pour in the egg yolk mixture.

4. Stir contents with a wooden spoon and cook until the temperature reaches 175°F, then remove from heat.

5. Pour the mixture into a clean bowl through a fine sieve in order to achieve a smooth, lump-free consistency.

6. Cover the bowl in plastic cling wrap, allow it to cool slightly, and then place it in the refrigerator for a minimum of 4 hours to ensure a very cold mixture.

7. Place remaining ½ cup whipping cream in a small pot and heat until boiling point. Remove from heat, add the chocolate and stir until chocolate is melted and a smooth uniform consistency is achieved.

8. Pour the cold ice cream mixture into an ice cream maker and run until the consistency is very firm.

9. Add the chocolate-cream mixture to the ice cream maker while the machine is working. Continue to run for another 2 minutes, allowing the ice cream to mix with the fudge, until preferred ice cream consistency is achieved – soft or firm.

Chocolate Brownie Bump Ice Cream

Makes

10

scoops

This is a rich double chocolate ice cream, chock-full of delicious brownie bits.

INGREDIENTS

½ cup milk

1½ cups whipping cream

1 teaspoon pure vanilla extract

¾ cup sugar

6 egg yolks

5 ounces bittersweet chocolate, at least 60% cocoa content

1 cup brownie chunks (store-bought or from the recipe on page 89)

I chose to use the French Vanilla Ice Cream (page 12) as a base in this recipe, but you can substitute others. If you choose to use the Italian Vanilla Ice Cream (page 11), reduce the amount of sugar in the recipe by two tablespoons.

PREPARATION

1. Place milk, cream, vanilla, and half the sugar in a saucepan and bring to a boil over medium heat.

2. Place egg yolks and the remaining sugar into a bowl and whisk together by hand until smooth and fully combined.

3. When the saucepan contents come to a boil, reduce heat and quickly pour in the egg yolk mixture.

4. Stir contents with a wooden spoon and cook until the temperature reaches 175°F, then remove from heat.

5. Pour the mixture into a clean bowl through a fine sieve in order to achieve a smooth, lump-free consistency.

6. Melt the chocolate in the microwave. Quickly add the melted chocolate into the mixture and stir.

7. Cover the bowl in plastic cling wrap, allow it to cool slightly, and then place it in the refrigerator for a minimum of 4 hours to ensure a very cold mixture.

8. Pour the mixture into an ice cream maker and run until the mixture is firm and just at the point of freezing. Add half the brownie chunks and run the machine for 1 minute.

9. Add the rest of the brownie chunks and run again until preferred ice cream consistency is achieved – soft or firm.

Candied Fruit Freak Ice Cream

Makes

12

scoops

This ice cream is inspired by the fruit layer of the classic southern Italian ice cream dish spumoni. A wonderful seasonal treat due to its bright colors, this is a fun ice cream to serve with candied fruit-filled Christmas cake.

INGREDIENTS

1½ cups milk

1 cup whipping cream

1 teaspoon pure vanilla extract

⅔ cup sugar

6 egg yolks

1 cup candied fruit (assorted)

1 tablespoon brandy

PREPARATION

1. Place milk, cream, vanilla, and half the sugar in a saucepan and bring to a boil over medium heat.

2. Place egg yolks and the remaining sugar into a bowl and whisk together by hand until smooth and fully combined.

3. When the saucepan contents come to a boil, reduce heat and quickly pour in the egg yolk mixture.

4. Stir contents with a wooden spoon and cook until the temperature reaches 175°F, then remove from heat.

5. Pour the mixture into a clean bowl through a fine sieve in order to achieve a smooth, lump-free consistency.

6. Add the candied fruit and brandy. Cover the bowl in plastic cling wrap and allow it to cool slightly.

7. Place the mixture in the refrigerator for a minimum of 4 hours to ensure a very cold mixture.

8. Pour the mixture into an ice cream maker and run until preferred ice cream consistency is achieved – soft or firm.

Ice Cream Toppings and Sauces

Really Vanilla Sauce

·

Light Chocolate Sauce

·

Caramel Sauce

·

Hot Chocolate Fudge

·

Praline Fudge

·

Peanut Butter Fudge

·

Rose Scented Pomegranate Sauce

·

Orange Pineapple Sauce

·

Rich Coffee Sauce

·

Rich Lemon Sauce

·

Berry Sauce

·

Rich Coconut Sauce

·

Butterscotch Sauce

Really Vanilla Sauce

Makes

3

cups

This classic sauce can be used as a base for various other flavors. The delicate texture and balance between sweetness and airiness makes for an especially high quality vanilla sauce.

INGREDIENTS

2 cups milk

½ cup sugar

1 vanilla bean, slit lengthwise, or
2 teaspoons pure vanilla extract

6 egg yolks

PREPARATION

1. Place milk, half the sugar, and the vanilla in a small saucepan and bring to a boil over medium heat.

2. In the meantime, place the egg yolks and the rest of the sugar in a separate bowl and whip until the mixture is smooth.

3. When the saucepan contents come to a boil, reduce heat to as low as possible. Quickly add ⅓ of the saucepan contents to the egg yolk mixture and whisk continuously until fully combined.

4. Continuing to whisk, add the remaining hot milk mixture to the whipped egg yolks.

5. Transfer bowl contents to saucepan. Continue cooking on low heat while stirring with a wooden spoon until the mixture reaches 175°F.

6. Remove from the heat and pour into a clean bowl through a sieve.

7. Place the bowl on top of another bowl filled with ice for 10 minutes or until the mixture reaches room temperature. Cover the bowl with plastic cling wrap and chill in the refrigerator for a minimum of 2 hours.

8. The sauce can be kept for up to 2 days in an airtight container.

9. Serve the sauce cold after a few hours in the refrigerator.

Light Chocolate Sauce

This is my version of a classic chocolate sauce – it does wonders in transforming a regular scoop of ice cream into a delectable dessert.

INGREDIENTS

2 cups milk

½ cup sugar

1 vanilla bean, slit lengthwise, or
2 teaspoons pure vanilla extract

6 egg yolks

5 ounces quality bittersweet chocolate,
minimum 50% cocoa content

2 teaspoons chocolate liqueur

PREPARATION

1. Place milk, half the sugar, and the vanilla in a small saucepan and bring to a boil over medium heat.

2. In the meantime, place the egg yolks and the rest of the sugar in a separate bowl and whip until the mixture is smooth.

3. When the saucepan contents come to a boil, reduce heat to as low as possible. Quickly add ⅓ of the saucepan contents to the egg yolk mixture and whisk continuously until fully combined.

4. Continuing to whisk, add the remaining hot milk mixture to the whipped egg yolks.

5. Transfer bowl contents to saucepan. Continue cooking on low heat while stirring with a wooden spoon until the mixture reaches 175°F.

6. Remove from the heat and add in the chocolate, combining with a handheld whisk until all the chocolate has melted into the mixture.

7. Pour into a clean bowl through a sieve. While the mixture is still hot, add the liqueur and stir.

8. Place the bowl on top of another bowl filled with ice for 10 minutes or until the mixture reaches room temperature. Cover the bowl and chill in the refrigerator for a minimum of 2 hours.

9. The sauce can be stored in an airtight container in the refrigerator for up to 2 days.

10. Serve the sauce cold after a few hours in the refrigerator.

Caramel Sauce

Makes

3

cups

This classic caramel sauce has been a favorite of mine for over 20 years. It's rich in flavor, easy to make, and always earns me loads of compliments!

INGREDIENTS

½ cup sugar

2 tablespoons water

1 cup whipping cream

PREPARATION

1. Place sugar and water in a medium sized saucepan and cook over medium heat until the sugar caramelizes to a golden brown. There is no need to stir at this stage.

2. Reduce heat and add the cream. Continue cooking while stirring with a wooden spoon until the sauce thickens slightly and absorbs all the sugar crystals that were produced as a result of the impact of the cold cream. Remove saucepan from heat.

3. Allow the sauce to cool to room temperature, then transfer to an airtight container and store in the refrigerator for up to 5 days.

4. Serve the sauce at room temperature.

Hot Chocolate Fudge

Makes

3

cups

If you seek the deepest, darkest depths of chocolate, this rich strong sauce is for you. It will wow even the most dedicated chocolate lovers.

INGREDIENTS

⅔ cup whipping cream

¼ cup milk

¼ cup sugar

½ pound bittersweet chocolate, cut into small pieces

PREPARATION

1. Pour the cream, milk, and sugar into a small saucepan and bring to a boil over medium heat.

2. Place the chocolate in a bowl and pour the boiling mixture over it. Stir the contents until all the chocolate has melted into the mixture.

3. Cover the mixture and allow it to cool to room temperature.

4. Transfer to an airtight container and refrigerate.

5. The sauce can only be used once it has hardened. It can be stored in the refrigerator in an airtight container for up to 1 week.

6. Serve the sauce hot, heated to at least 120°F.

Praline Fudge

Makes

4

cups

If you are as nuts for hazelnuts as I am you will love this sauce. It's rich in flavor with a heavy texture, just as a fudge sauce should be.

INGREDIENTS

1 cup whipping cream

¼ cup milk

½ cup hazelnut praline paste (not the same as hazelnut butter, praline paste is available at most specialty baking supply shops)

¼ cup sugar

½ pound bittersweet chocolate, cut into small pieces

PREPARATION

1. Place cream, milk, praline paste, and sugar in a small saucepan and bring to boiling point over medium heat.

2. Place chocolate in a bowl and pour hot mixture over it. Stir until all the chocolate has melted into the mixture, cover the bowl and allow the mixture to cool to room temperature.

3. Transfer mixture to an airtight container and place in the refrigerator. The sauce can only be used once it has hardened. Store it in the refrigerator in an airtight container for up to 1 week.

4. Serve the sauce at room temperature.

Peanut Butter Fudge

Makes

4

cups

I like to pair this sauce with simple, delicately flavored ice creams to allow the peanut butter fudge to take its rightful dominant place in the dessert.

INGREDIENTS

1 cup whipping cream

¼ cup milk

PREPARATION

1. Place cream, milk, peanut butter, and sugar in a small saucepan and bring to boiling point over medium heat.

½ cup peanut butter

¼ cup sugar

½ pound bittersweet chocolate, cut into small pieces

2. Place chocolate in a bowl and pour hot mixture over it. Stir until all the chocolate has melted into the mixture.

3. Cover the bowl and allow the mixture to cool to room temperature, then transfer to an airtight container and place in the refrigerator. The sauce can only be used once it has hardened. It can be stored in the refrigerator in an airtight container for up to 1 week.

4. Serve the sauce at room temperature.

Rose Scented Pomegranate Sauce

Makes

1½

cups

This sauce originates in Turkey, where rose water is widely used in a whole range of different recipes.

INGREDIENTS

½ cup sugar

2 tablespoons water

1 cup pomegranate juice

2 teaspoons rose water extract

This is a very subtle sauce, so it's important to pair it with an equally delicately flavored cake or ice cream; otherwise the special flavor of the rosewater will be lost. Rose water extract can be found in Asian, Indian, Pakistani, Mediterranean or Middle Eastern grocers.

PREPARATION

1. Place sugar and water in a medium sized saucepan and cook over medium heat until the sugar is almost caramelized. There is no need to stir at this stage.

2. Reduce heat and add the pomegranate juice. Continue cooking while stirring, until the sauce thickens slightly. Remove from the heat and add in the rose water extract.

3. Allow the sauce to cool completely, transfer to an airtight container and store in the refrigerator for up to 5 days.

4. This sauce is served completely cold after a few hours in the refrigerator.

Orange Pineapple Sauce

Makes

3

cups

The combination of pineapple and orange creates a refreshing summery flavor from predominantly winter fruits.

INGREDIENTS

½ cup sugar

2 tablespoons water

½ cup natural pineapple juice

½ cup natural orange juice

1 tablespoon cornstarch

2 teaspoons orange liqueur

This sauce goes well with various types of desserts, especially fruit desserts, and can also be used to spruce up day-old cakes that have dried out a little.

PREPARATION

1. Place sugar and water in a medium sized saucepan and cook over medium heat until the sugar is almost caramelized. There is no need to stir at this stage.

2. Reduce the heat and add the pineapple juice, orange juice, and cornstarch. Continue cooking while stirring with a wooden spoon until the sauce thickens slightly. Remove from heat and add in the orange liqueur.

3. Allow the sauce to cool to room temperature, then transfer to an airtight container. It can be stored in the refrigerator for up to 5 days.

4. Serve the sauce at room temperature.

Rich Coffee Sauce

Makes 2 cups

This coffee sauce is very concentrated and of very high quality, therefore it should be served in an appropriate quantity. In my opinion, coffee is a flavor that should be kept separate from other flavors; otherwise the taste is lost.

INGREDIENTS

½ cup sugar

2 tablespoons water

1 cup milk

½ cup butter

2 tablespoons quality instant coffee

2 teaspoons coffee liqueur

PREPARATION

1. Place sugar and water in a medium sized saucepan and cook over medium heat until the sugar is almost caramelized. There is no need to stir at this stage.

2. Reduce the heat, then add the milk, butter, and coffee. Continue cooking while stirring with a wooden spoon, until the sauce thickens slightly.

3. Remove from heat, add in the coffee liqueur and stir.

4. Allow the sauce to cool completely, then transfer to an airtight container and store in the refrigerator for up to 5 days.

5. Serve the sauce completely cold after a few hours in the refrigerator.

Rich Lemon Sauce

Makes

3

cups

Lemon is one of the most important ingredients in making sorbets and other desserts. A couple of drops of fresh lemon will strengthen the aroma of any other fruit during the freezing process.

INGREDIENTS

⅔ cup sugar

2 tablespoons water

1 cup freshly squeezed lemon juice

1 tablespoon cornstarch

2 teaspoons lemon zest

PREPARATION

1. Place sugar and water in a medium sized saucepan and cook over medium heat until the sugar is almost caramelized. There is no need to stir at this stage.

2. Reduce the heat, then add the lemon juice and the cornstarch. Continue cooking while stirring with a wooden spoon, until the sauce thickens slightly.

3. Remove from heat and add in the lemon zest.

4. Allow the sauce to cool completely, then transfer to an airtight container and store in the refrigerator for up to 5 days.

5. Serve the sauce completely cold after a few hours in the refrigerator.

Berry Sauce

Makes
3
cups

This is another classic. A gorgeous balance between sweet and tart, this light sauce goes well with either vanilla or chocolate.

INGREDIENTS

1 cup water

1 cup sugar

1 pound fresh or frozen mixed berries

1 teaspoon fresh lemon juice

PREPARATION

1. In a large saucepan, heat the water and sugar over high heat until boiling point, stirring occasionally.

2. In the meantime, if you are using frozen berries defrost them.

3. Place the berries and lemon juice in the blender. Pour in the water and sugar mixture, blending until the sauce is smooth.

4. Transfer the mixture to a bowl through a sieve.

5. The sauce can be kept in the refrigerator in an airtight container for up to 4 days.

6. Serve the sauce at room temperature.

Rich Coconut Sauce

Makes

2½

cups

The world is divided into two types of people—those who love coconut and those who don't. The former will love this sauce! Its heavy coconut taste lends it a somewhat Caribbean or Asian touch.

INGREDIENTS

½ cup sugar

2 tablespoons water

2 cups coconut milk

2 tablespoons shredded coconut

2 teaspoons coconut liqueur

PREPARATION

1. Place sugar and water in a medium sized saucepan and cook over medium heat until the sugar is almost caramelized. There is no need to stir at this stage.

2. Reduce the heat, then add the coconut milk and the shredded coconut. Continue cooking while stirring with a wooden spoon, until the sauce thickens slightly.

3. Remove from heat, add in the coconut liqueur and stir.

4. Allow the sauce to cool completely, then transfer to an airtight container and store in the refrigerator for up to 5 days.

5. Serve the sauce completely cold after a few hours in the refrigerator.

Butterscotch Sauce

Makes

1½

cups

This is my version of the familiar and well-loved sauce for ice creams and pies. It can be kept in the fridge for up to 3 days, but be sure to serve it at room temperature.

INGREDIENTS

1 cup brown sugar

¼ cup sweetened condensed milk

2 tablespoons light corn syrup, or honey

¼ cup butter

Pinch of salt

1 tablespoon espresso, or strong coffee

PREPARATION

1. In a small saucepan, over low heat, stir together the brown sugar and milk.

2. Add the corn syrup, butter, and salt. Continue to stir.

3. Add the coffee and warm until smooth and uniform; do not boil as it will cause the texture to break.

4. Serve at room temperature.

Sorbets

Tips and Techniques

·

Base Sugar Syrup for Sorbet

·

Pretty Pear Sorbet

·

Granny Green Apple Sorbet

·

White Peachy Keen Sorbet

·

Tequila Lime Shot Sorbet

·

Orange Brandy Sorbet

·

Black Forest Cherry Sorbet

·

Cantaloupe Cool Sorbet

·

Mango Madness Sorbet

·

Apricot Almond Indulgence Sorbet

·

Pomegranate Punch Sorbet

·

Cachaça Passion Sorbet

·

Blue-berriness Sorbet

·

Pineapple Rum Ball Sorbet

Tips and Techniques

- The base for every sorbet is sugar syrup (see opposite page).

- This chapter lists a number of recommended versions of sorbet that can be made using the syrup.

- In this chapter, each recipe is specifically suited to the type of fruit called for, according to the sugar content of the ripe fruit. If you choose to make the sorbet from frozen fruit, the amount of syrup must be increased. To be sure you've got it right, taste the mixture when it's cold, right before you pour it into the ice cream maker. The taste should be sweeter than that of ripe fruit because some of the sweetness is lost during the freezing process.

- Alcohol accentuates the sorbet flavor. That said, in all recipes that call for alcohol, the amount of alcohol can be easily reduced to your taste, or eliminated altogether. The correct ratio is 1 teaspoon alcohol for every cup of mix (syrup + fruit). If you use more alcohol, you will alter the freezing point and the mixture won't become a sorbet.

- Make the fruit purée in the blender. Blend small pieces of fruit in the blender without adding any liquid—the water content in the fruit is sufficient.

SERVING

- Sorbet is usually served as a refreshing end to a heavy meal. You can combine 2-3 scoops of different flavors to serve as dessert, top with fruit salad, or serve it as a fun, light addition to a richer dessert.

- Tarter or sour sorbets can be served in between courses of a multi-course meal to act as a palate cleanser. In this case, serve one small scoop per person.

- Serve sorbet to the kids in a cone on a hot day—just don't forget to cut out the alcohol.

- Sorbet can also be placed in a popsicle tray as soon as it´s ready. Just leave it in the freezer for 4 hours before serving.

- Sorbet can keep in the freezer for at least 2 weeks. If the flavor needs a bit of refreshing, defrost the sorbet and run it through the ice cream maker again.

- Sugar can be substituted with any type of low-calorie sweetener, but the glucose in the Base Sugar Syrup (see opposite page) cannot be omitted or substituted.

Base Sugar Syrup for Sorbet

Makes
5
cups

I highly recommend that you prepare this syrup in advance. It can be stored in the refrigerator in an airtight container for up to a month.

INGREDIENTS

2 cups water

3 cups sugar

¼ cup glucose

Glucose, which is called for in the recipe, comes in liquid form and can be found in specialty baking stores.

PREPARATION

1. Place all ingredients in a pot and cook till boiling point.

2. Remove from heat and cool to room temperature.

3. Place in the refrigerator and chill for at least 1 hour prior to using.

Pretty Pear Sorbet

Makes
10
cups

This special richly flavored sorbet holds its own as a main dessert. I like to use Bartlett pears to make this sorbet because they are especially juicy and flavourful.

INGREDIENTS

1 cup sugar syrup (see above)

2 cups very ripe pears, finely puréed

1 teaspoon lemon juice

PREPARATION

1. Mix all the ingredients together in a bowl and place in the refrigerator for at least half an hour.

2. Pour the mixture into the ice cream maker and run until the texture is firm.

Granny Green Apple Sorbet

Makes
8
cups

This is a particularly refreshing sorbet. The tartness in the green apples makes this flavor a great palate cleanser. If you prefer a non-alcoholic sorbet, simply eliminate the alcohol and prepare the sorbet as instructed.

INGREDIENTS

1 cup sugar syrup (page 59)

1½ cups Granny Smith apples, finely puréed

1 teaspoon Calvados

1 teaspoon freshly squeezed lemon juice

PREPARATION

1. Mix all the ingredients together in a bowl and place in the refrigerator for at least half an hour.

2. Pour the mixture into the ice cream maker and run until the texture is firm.

White Peachy Keen Sorbet

Makes
10
cups

This sorbet has a very rich aroma. I recommend serving it at the end of a meal, either on its own, or alongside fruit pies. If you prefer a non-alcoholic sorbet, simply eliminate the alcohol and prepare the sorbet as instructed.

INGREDIENTS

1 cup sugar syrup (page 59)

1¾ cups white peaches, finely puréed

1 teaspoon peach schnapps

1 teaspoon freshly squeezed lemon juice

PREPARATION

1. Mix all the ingredients together in a bowl and place in the refrigerator for at least half an hour.

2. Pour the mixture into the ice cream maker and run until the texture is firm.

Granny Green Apple Sorbet

Tequila Lime Shot Sorbet

Tequila Lime Shot Sorbet

Makes **8** cups

A summery sorbet, this flavor is well suited to the hottest days of summer. This sorbet is also nice with fruit salad. If you prefer a non-alcoholic sorbet, simply eliminate the alcohol and prepare the sorbet as instructed.

INGREDIENTS

1 cup sugar syrup (page 59)

1 cup freshly squeezed lime juice

2 teaspoons gold tequila

I like to serve this sorbet at the end of a summery Mexican meal in a festive shot glass before dessert. It's perfect after a particularly spicy or aromatic meal.

PREPARATION

1. Mix all the ingredients together in a bowl and place in the refrigerator for at least half an hour.

2. Pour the mixture into the ice cream maker and run until the texture is firm.

Orange Brandy Sorbet

Makes **10** cups

This sorbet can be a nice mid-course palate cleanser, or a light dessert for a particularly heavy meal. If you prefer a non-alcoholic sorbet, simply eliminate the alcohol and prepare the sorbet as instructed.

INGREDIENTS

1 cup sugar syrup (page 59)

1¼ cups freshly squeezed orange juice

2 teaspoons quality brandy liqueur

PREPARATION

1. Mix all the ingredients together in a bowl and place in the refrigerator for at least half an hour.

2. Pour the mixture into the ice cream maker and run until the texture is firm.

Black Forest Cherry Sorbet

Makes **10** cups

This sorbet is great for a light dessert atop a bowl of fruit salad or as a accompaniment to a slice of chocolate cake. If you prefer a non-alcoholic sorbet, simply eliminate the alcohol and prepare the sorbet as instructed.

INGREDIENTS

1 cup sugar syrup (page 59)

1¾ cups black cherries, finely puréed

1 teaspoon cherry liqueur

1 teaspoon freshly squeezed lemon juice

PREPARATION

1. Mix all the ingredients together in a bowl and place in the refrigerator for at least half an hour.

2. Pour the mixture into the ice cream maker and run until the texture is firm.

Cantaloupe Cool Sorbet

Makes **8** cups

This sorbet is perfect for making popsicles for kids – just eliminate the alcohol and prepare the sorbet as instructed. See Mango Popsicle on page 91 for popsicle making instructions.

INGREDIENTS

1 cup sugar syrup (page 59)

1½ cups sweet ripe cantaloupe, finely puréed

1 teaspoon melon schnapps

1 teaspoon freshly squeezed lemon juice

PREPARATION

1. Mix all the ingredients together in a bowl and place in the refrigerator for at least half an hour.

2. Pour the mixture into the ice cream maker and run until the texture is firm.

Black Forest Cherry Sorbet

Mango Madness Sorbet

Mango Madness Sorbet

Makes

10

cups

During the freezing process, the sorbet takes on this amazing, refreshing flavor, which is why both kids and adults alike love it. If you and your kids are mango fans, see page 91 for how to turn this sorbet into popsicles.

INGREDIENTS

1 cup sugar syrup (page 59)

1½ cups under-ripe mango, peeled and finely puréed. (Use mango that is not quite ripe. If it's completely ripe, the sorbet will be too sweet.)

1 teaspoon freshly squeezed lemon juice

PREPARATION

1. Mix all the ingredients together in a bowl and place in the refrigerator for at least half an hour.

2. Pour the mixture into the ice cream maker and run until the texture is firm.

Apricot Almond Indulgence Sorbet

Makes

10

cups

This sorbet is excellent served with a slice of hot cake—right after it comes out of the oven! If you prefer a non-alcoholic sorbet, simply eliminate the alcohol and prepare the sorbet as instructed.

INGREDIENTS

1 cup sugar syrup (page 59)

1¾ cups fresh ripe apricots, finely puréed

1 teaspoon amaretto

1 teaspoon freshly squeezed lemon juice

PREPARATION

1. Mix all the ingredients together in a bowl and place in the refrigerator for at least half an hour.

2. Pour the mixture into the ice cream maker and run until the texture is firm.

Pomegranate Punch Sorbet

Makes
10
cups

This very special sorbet features the uniquely sweet yet tart flavor of pomegranate. If you prefer a non-alcoholic sorbet, simply eliminate the alcohol and prepare the sorbet as instructed.

INGREDIENTS

1 cup sugar syrup (page 59)

1¼ cups freshly squeezed (or store bought) pomegranate juice

1 teaspoon Triple Sec

PREPARATION

1. Mix all the ingredients together in a bowl and place in the refrigerator for at least half an hour.

2. Pour the mixture into the ice cream maker and run until the texture is firm.

Cachaça Passion Sorbet

Makes
10
cups

This sorbet has a particularly tropical flavor. It goes well with Caribbean dishes. If you prefer a non-alcoholic sorbet, simply eliminate the alcohol and prepare the sorbet as instructed.

INGREDIENTS

1 cup sugar syrup (page 59)

1½ cups passion fruit pulp (with seeds)

2 teaspoons Cachaça liqueur

PREPARATION

1. Mix all the ingredients together in a bowl and place in the refrigerator for at least half an hour.

2. Pour the mixture into the ice cream maker and run until the texture is firm.

Pomegranate Punch Sorbet

Blue-berriness Sorbet

Blue-berriness Sorbet

Makes 10 cups

This sorbet is a favorite with kids, who are attracted to its deep color. If you prefer a non-alcoholic sorbet, simply eliminate the alcohol and prepare the sorbet as instructed.

INGREDIENTS

1 cup sugar syrup (page 59)

1¼ cups blueberries, finely puréed

1 teaspoon cherry liqueur

1 teaspoon freshly squeezed lemon juice

PREPARATION

1. Mix all the ingredients together in a bowl and place in the refrigerator for at least half an hour.

2. Pour the mixture into the ice cream maker and run until the texture is firm.

Pineapple Rum Ball Sorbet

Makes 10 cups

The combination of fresh pineapple and rum is what makes this sorbet a winner! If you prefer a non-alcoholic sorbet, simply eliminate the alcohol and prepare the sorbet as instructed.

INGREDIENTS

1 cup sugar syrup (page 59)

1½ cups ripe pineapple, finely puréed

2 teaspoons dark rum

1 teaspoon freshly squeezed lemon juice

PREPARATION

1. Mix all the ingredients together in a bowl and place in the refrigerator for at least half an hour.

2. Pour the mixture into the ice cream maker and run until the texture is firm.

Ice Cream Desserts

Banana Split

•

Belgian Waffle

•

Chocolate Log with Vanilla Ice Cream and Berries

•

Grilled Peaches with Amaretto Sauce and
Mediterranean Marzipan Ice Cream

•

Baked Pears with Vanilla Ice Cream and Caramel

•

Vanilla Pavlova with Vanilla Ice Cream and Berry Sauce

•

Ice Cream Sandwiches

•

Brownie Sundae with Vanilla Ice Cream and Hot Chocolate Sauce

•

Mango Popsicle

•

Donuts filled with Ice Cream and Berry Sauce

Banana Split

Serves

3

Classic desserts earn their status for a reason. That couldn't be truer than of the banana split—the Rolls Royce of ice cream sundaes.

INGREDIENTS

⅓ cup sugar

3 large ripe bananas, cut into 4 equal pieces

¼ cup of butter

1 scoop vanilla ice cream per serving (see recipes on pages 11-13)

PREPARATION

1. Place the sugar in a Teflon pan and cook over medium heat until the sugar caramelizes to a light brown. Stir occasionally with a wooden spoon, taking care not to burn.

2. Add the bananas and fry, carefully flipping over with a fork, until they turn a golden brown on all sides.

3. As soon as the bananas are ready, quickly transfer them to deep serving dishes and place the pan back on the heat.

4. Add the butter to the pan. Cook while stirring with a wooden spoon, until the sauce is brown.

5. Place a scoop of vanilla ice cream on top of the bananas and serve. For added richness, top with a spoonful of sauce.

Belgian Waffle

Makes

This waffle can be served with a variety of ice cream, fruit, and syrup or sauce toppings.

INGREDIENTS

1 cup milk

¼ cup sugar

4 eggs

½ teaspoon salt

¼ teaspoon vanilla extract

¾ cup flour

½ cup melted butter

8 scoops ice cream, any flavor

Try this recipe with: fresh strawberries and vanilla ice cream, banana ice cream and slices of bananas fried in butter and sugar, chocolate ice cream, or any other combination you can come up with.

PREPARATION

1. Place milk, sugar, eggs, salt, and vanilla in the bowl of an electric mixer and run on low speed. Slowly add half the amount of flour while the mixer is running and continue mixing for 3 minutes.

2. Keeping the mixer running, add the butter and the rest of the flour and mix until the dough is smooth and shiny.

3. Transfer the dough to a clean bowl and cover in cling wrap.

4. Place in the refrigerator for at least 30 minutes.

5. Remove the dough from the refrigerator and divide into 4 equal portions. Form each portion into a ball.

6. Place the ball of dough in the waffle iron and press down.

7. Bake the waffles until they turn golden brown.

8. Serve hot with the ice cream of your choice. For added indulgence top ice cream with hot chocolate sauce.

Chocolate Log with Vanilla Ice Cream and Berries

Serves

This is another classic dessert that reminds me of the tiny neighborhood pâtisserie I used to frequent in Paris.

INGREDIENTS

Dough

4 egg whites

⅔ cup sugar

4 egg yolks

⅓ cup flour

2 tablespoons cocoa

3 tablespoons powdered sugar

Filling

Vanilla ice cream of your choice (halved recipe; see pages 11-13)

½ pound of fresh berries

PREPARATION

1. Place the egg whites in the bowl of an electric mixer and beat until they form soft peaks. Slowly add half the sugar and continue beating until egg whites form stiff peaks.

2. Transfer the mixture to a larger bowl and place the egg yolks in the electric mixer bowl (no need to wash the bowl). Beat the yolks with the remaining sugar until they form stiff peaks. Add the egg yolk mixture to the egg white mixture.

3. Sift a third of the flour onto the mixture and fold everything together using a rubber spatula. Once the flour has been thoroughly combined, add the rest of the flour and the cocoa. Continue folding until the mixture is smooth and uniform.

4. Prepare a baking tray lined with parchment paper. Using a large knife or a long palette knife, spread on a ¼-inch layer of batter. Top with powdered sugar and put in a 375°F preheated oven for 12 minutes.

5. Remove the cake from the tray (with the parchment paper) and place on a wire rack to cool.

6. Flip the cake over onto a work surface and carefully peel off the parchment paper. Keep the cake bottom side-up and spread with ice cream. Scatter the berries and roll lengthwise.

7. Immediately place the roll in the freezer for at least 1 hour.

8. To serve, remove the roll from the freezer and slice into inch-wide slices. You can also top each slice with melted chocolate before serving.

Grilled Peaches with Amaretto Sauce and Mediterranean Marzipan Ice Cream

Serves

 6

I first ate this magnificent dessert in a small trattoria in northern Italy a number of years ago. It was one of the first desserts I made upon returning home.

INGREDIENTS

6 large ripe yellow peaches, pitted and quartered

2 tablespoons amaretto liqueur

¼ cup sugar

4 ounces soft butter

¼ cup water

Mediterranean Marzipan Ice Cream (halved recipe; see page 22)

Equipment

Grill pan

PREPARATION

1. Heat the grill pan over high heat.

2. Once the pan is hot, place peaches face down in the pan.

3. Grill the peaches for a few minutes until grill marks are visible on the side touching the pan. Repeat on the other side of the quarter.

4. Transfer peaches to a bowl and immediately top with 1 tablespoon of the amaretto liqueur, then lightly stir.

5. Place sugar and butter in a small saucepan and cook over medium heat until the caramel is golden.

6. Add ¼ cup water and the remaining amaretto to the saucepan and continue cooking for another 2-3 minutes until the mixture is smooth and uniform. Do not stir.

7. Place 4 peach quarters on 6 individual serving plates.

8. Pour the remaining peach liquid into the saucepan and stir.

9. Place a small scoop of marzipan ice cream on each dish of peaches, then top with a tablespoon of sauce.

Baked Pears with Vanilla Ice Cream and Caramel

Serves

This is an elegant, tasty and impressive dessert, well-suited to a festive holiday meal or a chic dinner party.

INGREDIENTS

½ cup sugar

2 tablespoons water

2 tablespoons butter

6 large, almost ripe pears (peel and slice in half lengthwise, remove seeds and slice each half into 3 pieces, also lengthwise)

Italian Vanilla Ice Cream (halved recipe; see page 11)

PREPARATION

1. Place sugar and water in a wide saucepan and cook until the caramel is golden brown. Add the butter and pears.

2. Reduce heat and continue cooking until the pears turn golden brown. Carefully turn the pears over occasionally.

3. Transfer the pears to a bowl and allow them to cool to room temperature.

4. Transfer the pears to the refrigerator for at least 30 minutes.

5. To create a dessert for sharing, arrange the pears in a fan-like fashion and top with a large scoop of ice cream. For added panache garnish with a vanilla bean (as shown in photo), or drizzle with remaining sauce.

6. An individual serving option is to pour the liquid remaining in the saucepan into a deep serving dish, place the pears arched side down and top each piece of pear with a small scoop of ice cream.

Vanilla Pavlova with Vanilla Ice Cream and Berry Sauce

Makes

8

Simple, natural and delicious, this recipe will have meringue fans coming back for seconds.

INGREDIENTS

3 egg whites

½ cup sugar

French Vanilla Ice Cream (halved recipe; see page 12)

Berry Sauce (halved recipe; see page 53)

Fresh berries (raspberries, blueberries, or both, for topping)

Equipment

Baking tray lined with parchment paper

This homemade version of pavlova is made easier by eliminating the need for a piping bag.

PREPARATION

1. Place the egg whites in the bowl of an electric mixer and beat on high speed until soft and fluffy.

2. Slowly add the sugar while continuing to beat, until egg whites form stiff peaks.

3. Using a spoon, place large egg white mounds (3 inches in diameter) on the parchment lined tray. The mounds should be spaced ½ inch apart.

4. Place in a preheated 300°F oven for 1 hour.

5. Remove tray from the oven and cool meringues for 30 minutes on a wire rack.

6. To serve, place each meringue on an individual serving dish and top with a small scoop of vanilla ice cream, some berry sauce, and a handful of fresh berries.

Ice Cream Sandwiches

Makes

8

An ice cream truck and corner store favorite, ice cream sandwiches inspire childhood memories of summertime fun. I decided to give this classic treat a facelift, resulting in an elegant reinvention.

INGREDIENTS

2 eggs

½ cup sugar

6 ounces bittersweet chocolate

½ cup butter

¼ cup flour

2 tablespoons cocoa

¾ cup chocolate chips

Vanilla ice cream (halved recipe; see pages 11-13)

Equipment

Baking tray lined with parchment paper

PREPARATION

1. Place eggs and sugar in the bowl of an electric mixer and beat until stiff peaks are formed.

2. Place chocolate and butter in a separate bowl and melt over a pot of boiling water (double boiler).

3. Add the melted chocolate to the egg and sugar mixture and whisk by hand until the mixture is smooth and uniform.

4. Add the flour and the cocoa and continue whisking by hand until the mixture is smooth and uniform.

5. Place a tablespoonful of the batter on the parchment lined baking try and, using the spoon, smear out to form a large teardrop shape, about 4 inches long. The base should be 1½ inches wide, while the other end should be narrower. You can also form whatever shape you like, or use variously shaped baking rings in which you place the batter. Make 16-20 biscuits, spaced ½ inch apart.

6. Sprinkle chocolate chips over the cookie batter.

7. Place tray in a preheated 375°F oven for 12 minutes.

8. Remove tray from oven and allow the biscuits to cool for at least 20 minutes at room temperature, then place in the refrigerator for 30 minutes.

9. Once the biscuits have cooled thoroughly, take a biscuit, top with ice cream and then cover with a second biscuit to create an ice cream sandwich. Immediately place in the freezer for 20 minutes. The sandwiches can be stored in the freezer for up to 4 days.

10. Serve the sandwiches straight from the freezer.

Brownie Sundae with Vanilla Ice Cream and Hot Chocolate Sauce

Makes

12

This traditional New York-born sundae undergoes a slight renovation. This is a great dessert for the kids to help assemble.

INGREDIENTS

Brownies

12 ounces bittersweet chocolate

1 cup butter

5 eggs

¾ cup sugar

½ cup flour

Chocolate Sauce

½ cup whipping cream

2 tablespoons sugar

4 ounces bittersweet chocolate

Vanilla ice cream (halved recipe; see pages 11-13)

Equipment

One 9x12 inch baking pan lined with parchment paper

PREPARATION

1. Prepare brownies: melt chocolate and butter in bowl placed over a pot of boiling water (double boiler).

2. Beat eggs and sugar in an electric mixer until stiff peaks form.

3. Once the chocolate and butter have melted, remove from heat. Slowly add the flour, combining with a rubber spatula.

4. Fold in the beaten eggs and sugar with a rubber spatula.

5. When the mixture is uniform, transfer to baking pan.

6. Place the baking pan in a preheated 350°F oven for 12 minutes. Remove from oven and place on wire rack to cool for 30 minutes, then into the refrigerator for a minimum of 2 hours.

7. Once cool, remove the brownies from the pan (with parchment paper still attached) and set down on a work surface. Using a sharp knife, slice the brownies into 3-inch square pieces. Wipe the knife with a wet cloth between cuts and peel the parchment paper off each brownie.

8. Prepare sauce: heat whipping cream and sugar in a saucepan over medium heat until boiling point. Once the cream is boiling, reduce heat, add chocolate and whisk continuously to ensure the mixture is lump-free.

9. Place each brownie on an individual serving dish, top with a scoop of vanilla ice cream and then pour on the hot chocolate sauce. To create a dessert for sharing, create a triple-decker brownie and ice cream sandwich. Serve immediately.

Mango Popsicle

Mango Popsicle

Makes

These are excellent on a hot summer day—each bite is pure pleasure. They make a great snack for kids and an equally tempting treat for grown-ups.

INGREDIENTS

Mango Madness Sorbet (see page 67), follow recipe to create only a soft sorbet

PREPARATION

1. While the sorbet in the ice cream maker is still soft, transfer to the ice cream bar molds. Fill right to the top and quickly stick in a popsicle stick.

2. Immediately place mold in freezer, ensuring that it is standing vertically, and freeze for at least 24 hours.

Donuts filled with Vanilla Ice Cream and Berry Sauce

Serves

In this recipe you will elevate store bought donuts from breakfast on-the-go status to a dessert dish. This is also a great dessert to let the kids assemble once you've sliced the donuts in half.

INGREDIENTS

2 tablespoons butter

2 tablespoons sugar

4 fresh donuts, sliced in half

Vanilla ice cream (halved recipe; see pages 11-13)

Berry Sauce (halved recipe; see page 53)

PREPARATION

1. Place butter and sugar in a Teflon pan and cook over medium heat until caramel starts to form. Place the halved donuts facedown in the pan, fry for 2 minutes and then transfer to a large plate to cool slightly.

2. On a serving plate, place bottom of each donut, cover with a scoop of ice cream and then cover with donut top. Pour berry sauce into the donut hole and serve immediately.

Ice Cream Cakes

Tips and Techniques

•

Chocolate Fudge Ice Cream Tart

•

Caramel and Crumble Vanilla Ice Cream Cake

•

Apricot and Cherry Ice Cream Cake

•

Candied Pecan and Peanut Butter Explosion Ice Cream Tart

•

Frozen Tiramisu

•

Chocolate Torte with Raspberry Mousse

•

Berry Vanilla Bramble Ice Cream Tart

Tips and Techniques

Ice cream cakes are perfect for special occasions—they add a certain whimsy and excitement to any event. To select and make the perfect ice cream cake, read the recipes in advance, get your ingredients together and make sure to time the preparations appropriately, especially having the ice cream at the right consistency ready in the ice cream maker when you need it. This will not only make things easier, but will result in a better cake.

Use these recipes as general guidelines and then let your imagination soar. Be creative, taking your personal taste into account. Don't hesitate to change certain ingredients or serving advice. Most importantly, enjoy the inherent fun in ice cream making.

• When making ice cream cakes, use fresh ice cream that's still soft from the ice cream maker.

• If you have already frozen ice cream, transfer it to the refrigerator for 15 minutes before using it to make your ice cream cake.

• Spring form pans—the pans specified in the recipes—are the best and easiest to use when making ice cream cakes.

• The quantities listed for the 10-inch spring form pan are generally equivalent to 3-4 individual 4-inch pans, depending on the cake.

• Before placing your finished cake in the freezer, you should straighten out the top layer of ice cream using a palette knife.

Chocolate Fudge Ice Cream Tart

Serves

An alternative name for this dish could be "Chocolate Punch-in-the-Face Pie". The rich and intensely chocolaty filling is served in a crisp, sweet piecrust.

INGREDIENTS

½ cup cold butter

3 tablespoons powdered sugar

1 egg

1 tablespoon cold water

½ teaspoon salt

1¼ cups flour

Chocolate Fudge Thud Ice Cream (see page 33)

Hot Chocolate Fudge (halved recipe; see page 45)

Equipment

One 10-inch tart pan, or four 4-inch individual-sized tart pans

Pie weights or dried beans

The dough can be kept in the freezer for up to 2 months. To defrost, remove from the freezer and allow it to defrost at room temperature.

PREPARATION

1. Place the butter and sugar in a food processor and run for 2 minutes until the mixture is smooth, stopping occasionally to scrape down the sides with a rubber spatula.

2. Stop the food processor and add the egg, water, and salt. Then run the processor for another 2 minutes until the mixture is smooth and uniform.

3. Stop the food processor again and add the flour. Run for 1 minute until a ball of dough is formed. Remove the ball from the food processor and cover with cling wrap. Place in the refrigerator for a minimum of 1 hour, or until ready for use.

4. On a floured work surface, roll out the dough to ⅛ inch thick, then transfer to a tart pan and mold into the pan using your fingers. Using a sharp knife, slice off any dough hanging over the side of the tart pan.

5. Once the dough is placed in the tart pan, line with aluminum foil. Weight down paper with pie weights or dried beans. Place in a preheated 375°F oven and bake for 20 to 25 minutes.

6. Remove the tart from the oven, quickly take off the aluminum foil and the weights or beans, and set aside. (You can re-use the foil and beans a number of times.) Place the tart pan on a wire rack to cool for 30 minutes.

7. To make tart: remove the piecrust from the tart pan and fill with scoops of ice cream, placed close together, until the entire crust is generously filled with chocolate ice cream. Pour on the chocolate fudge and serve immediately.

Caramel and Crumble Vanilla Ice Cream Cake

Makes

If chocolate isn't your thing and vanilla seems a bit boring, you must be a caramel lover! This cake takes things up a notch with the use of homemade caramel and crumble.

INGREDIENTS

Torte
4 egg whites

⅔ cup sugar

4 egg yolks

½ cup flour

3 tablespoons powdered sugar

Crumble
¼ cup butter

¼ cup flour

2 tablespoons powdered sugar

1 tablespoon milk

Vanilla ice cream (see recipes pages 11-13)

½ cup Caramel Sauce (see recipe page 43)

Equipment
Baking tray lined with parchment paper

4 individual-sized 3-inch spring form pans

PREPARATION

1. Prepare torte: place the egg whites in the bowl of an electric mixer and beat until soft peaks form.

2. Slowly add half the sugar and continue beating until stiff peaks form.

3. Transfer mixer contents to a larger bowl, and then add the egg yolks to the mixer (no need to wash the bowl).

4. Beat the egg yolks with the rest of the sugar until stiff peaks form.

5. Transfer to the bowl of egg whites, add a third of the flour and fold together with a rubber spatula.

6. Once the mixture is uniform, add the rest of the flour. Continue folding with the rubber spatula until the mixture is smooth and uniform.

7. Using a palette knife, spread the dough ¼ inch thick onto parchment paper lined baking tray.

8. Sprinkle with powdered sugar and place in a preheated 375°F oven for 12 minutes.

9. Remove from the oven and cool on a wire rack for 1 hour.

(continued on next page)

(continued from previous page)

10. Prepare crumble: place all the ingredients in a food processor that has a metal blade. Run the processor until contents take on a crumb-like texture.

11. Transfer the crumbs to a baking tray and place in a pre-heated 375°F oven for 15 minutes. (You may also bake the crumbs at the same time as the cake.)

12. Assemble cake: flip the cooled cake over onto a work surface and carefully peel off the parchment paper.

13. Place the bottom of one of the spring form pans on top of the cake and, using a knife, cut out 12 circles the size of the pan.

14. Place a circle of cake inside each spring form pan and pour on 2 tablespoons of the ice cream still soft from the ice cream maker. Place in the freezer for 30 minutes.

15. Remove the pans from the freezer, place a tablespoon of caramel in each spring pan and top with another circle of cake.

16. Pour on another 2 tablespoons of ice cream and return to the freezer for another 30 minutes.

17. Remove pans from the freezer and place 1 tablespoon of caramel, another circle of cake, and another 2 tablespoons of ice cream on each. Return to freezer for 15 minutes.

18. Using a spoon, place a small dollop of ice cream on the top layer of cake and return to the freezer for another 15 minutes.

19. Store the cake in the freezer for up to 1 week, or serve immediately.

20. To serve, remove the cakes from their spring form pans, roll in crumbs and then drizzle each cake with caramel sauce.

Apricot and Cherry Ice Cream Cake

This recipe is surely for the fruit lovers! The combination of two fruit ice creams is both lovely to look at and light and refreshing to the taste.

INGREDIENTS

4 egg whites

⅔ cup sugar

4 egg yolks

½ cup flour

3 tablespoons powdered sugar

Apricot Ape Ice Cream (see recipe page 14)

Black Forest Cherry Sorbet (see recipe page 64)

Equipment

Baking tray lined with parchment paper

One 7-inch high by 7-inch wide spring form pan

PREPARATION

1. Place the egg whites in the bowl of an electric mixer and beat until soft peaks form.

2. Slowly add half the sugar and continue beating until stiff peaks form.

3. Transfer mixer contents to a larger bowl, and then add the egg yolks to the mixer (no need to wash the bowl).

4. Beat the egg yolks with the rest of the sugar until stiff peaks form.

5. Transfer to the bowl of egg whites, add a third of the flour and fold together with a rubber spatula.

6. Once the mixture is uniform, add the rest of the flour and continue folding with the rubber spatula until the mixture is smooth and uniform.

7. Using a palette knife, spread the dough ¼ inch thick onto parchment paper lined baking tray.

8. Sprinkle with powdered sugar and place in a preheated 375°F oven for 12 minutes.

9. Remove from the oven and cool on a wire rack for 1 hour.

10. Flip the cake over onto a work surface and carefully peel off the parchment paper.

(continued on next page)

(continued from previous page)

11. Place the bottom of the spring form pan on top of the cake and, using a knife, cut out a circle the size of the pan. If possible, cut out a second circle. If not, keep the leftover pieces to use as the second cake layer.

12. Place the circle of cake inside the spring form pan and pour on the Apricot Ape Ice Cream still soft from the ice cream maker. Place in the freezer for 30 minutes.

13. Remove the pan from the freezer and top the ice cream with second circle of cake or pieces of the leftover cake.

14. Pour on the Black Forest Cherry Sorbet and place in the freezer for another 30 minutes.

15. Remove pan from the freezer, straighten out the top layer of ice cream, and return to freezer for another 15 minutes.

16. Store the cake in the freezer for up to 1 week, or serve immediately with fresh fruit (if in season).

Candied Pecan and Peanut Butter Explosion Ice Cream Tart

Serves

8

The secret to this pie's success is the crisp, sweet piecrust and sweet (but not too sweet) peanut butter ice cream.

INGREDIENTS

½ cup cold butter

3 tablespoons powdered sugar

1 egg

1 tablespoon cold water

½ teaspoon salt

1¼ cups flour

Candied Pecan and Peanut Butter Explosion Ice Cream (see page 30)

¼ cup peanut butter

Equipment

One 10-inch tart pan or four 4-inch individual sized tart pans

Pie weights or dried beans

Piping bag with a ¼ inch circular head

PREPARATION

1. Place the butter and sugar in a food processor and run for 2 minutes until the mixture is smooth, stopping occasionally to scrape down the sides with a rubber spatula.

2. Stop the food processor and add the egg, water and salt. Run for another 2 minutes until the mixture is smooth and uniform.

3. Stop the food processor again and add the flour. Run for 1 minute until a ball of dough is formed. Remove the ball from the food processor and cover with cling wrap. Place in the refrigerator for a minimum of 1 hour, or until ready for use.

4. The dough can be kept in the freezer for up to 2 months. To defrost, remove from the freezer and allow it to defrost at room temperature.

5. On a floured work surface, roll out the dough to ⅛ inch thick, then transfer to a tart pan and mold into pan using your fingers. Using a sharp knife, slice off any dough hanging over the side of the pan. If you're using the 4-inch pans, repeat this with the rest of the tart pans.

(continued on next page)

(continued from previous page)

6. Once the dough is placed in the tart pan, line with aluminum foil. Weight down paper with pie weights or dried beans. Place in a preheated 375°F oven and bake for 20-25 minutes.

7. Remove tart from the oven, quickly take off the aluminum foil and the weights or beans, and set aside. (You can re-use the foil and beans a number of times.) Place the tart pan on a wire rack to cool for half an hour.

8. Prepare tart: remove the piecrust from the tart pan and fill with scoops of peanut butter ice cream, placed close together, until the entire crust is generously filled with ice cream. Use a piping bag to drizzle on peanut butter topping. If you are using 4-inch plates, repeat the process.

Frozen Tiramisu

Makes

I've created a frozen version of what is probably the most famous Italian dessert. I highly recommend that you use freshly made espresso if possible, using an espresso machine or a macchinetta.

INGREDIENTS

⅔ cup sugar

3 tablespoons water

8 egg yolks

6 short shots of espresso

2 tablespoons amaretto liqueur

1 pound mascarpone cheese

1 cup whipping cream (whipped to stiff peaks with an electric mixer)

1 pound lady fingers

3 tablespoons cocoa

Equipment

4 square 4x4-inch spring form pans

Candy thermometer

Espresso machine or macchinetta

If you don't have an espresso machine or a macchinetta, you can try substituting very strong drip coffee. Note: 1 shot of espresso is equivalent to 1 ounce.

PREPARATION

1. Place sugar and water in a small saucepan and heat until boiling point.

2. In the meantime, place egg yolks in the bowl of an electric mixer and beat on maximum speed.

3. Once the sugar water has reached boiling point, continue cooking until it reaches 250°F (measure with candy thermometer – the exact temperature is important).

4. Slowly add the sugar water to the beaten eggs while the mixer is running. The result will be a light and airy bright yellow mixture. (The professional term for this mixture is sabayon).

5. Let the mixer continue running until the sabayon mixture is around room temperature.

6. In the meantime, prepare the espresso and transfer to a clean bowl.

7. Add the amaretto to the coffee and stir. Set aside.

8. In a separate large and wide dish, place the mascarpone cheese and whisk by hand to achieve a smooth, lump-free consistency.

9. Add the sabayon to the cheese and fold together using a rubber or silicon spatula until the consistency is uniform.

(continued on next page)

(continued from previous page)

10. Add the whipped cream and continue folding until the mixture is once again smooth and uniform.

11. To assemble the tiramisu: place each lady finger into the coffee mixture for 1 second, turn over, then lay 4 biscuits horizontally next to each other on the bottom of each spring form pan.

12. Continue dunking and placing 3 biscuits next to each other vertically along the pan walls. In total, 12 biscuits will line the 4 walls.

13. Place 5-6 tablespoons of the cream mixture into each pan, sprinkle with cocoa, then top with 3 more tablespoons of cream.

14. Place the pans in the freezer for a minimum of 2 hours— all night, if possible.

15. Remove pan walls and sprinkle with cocoa just before serving.

Chocolate Torte with Raspberry Mousse

Serves

This celebratory cake was one of the first I learned to make at "Le Cordon Bleu" in Paris. It was love at first sight!

Torte Dough

4 egg whites

½ cup sugar

4 egg yolks

½ cup flour

¼ cup cocoa

Raspberry Mousse

1 cup whipping cream

½ cup sugar

½ cup raspberries, puréed in a blender

1 teaspoon gelatin powder dissolved in 4 tablespoons boiling water

For Assembly

½ cup Berry Sauce (see page 53)

9 fresh raspberries for decoration

Equipment

Baking sheet lined with parchment paper

Piping bag with a ¼ inch circular head

PREPARATION

1. Beat the eggs whites in an electric mixer until consistency is creamy.

2. Slowly add half the sugar, while beating, until stiff peaks form. Transfer to a large bowl.

3. Beat the egg yolks and remaining sugar in an electric mixer until consistency is smooth. Add to the egg whites.

4. Add the flour and the cocoa and gently fold into the egg mixture with a rubber spatula until smooth.

5. Pour batter onto the parchment lined baking sheet and spread using a palette knife to achieve an even height.

6. Place baking sheet in 375°F preheated oven and bake for 15 minutes.

7. Remove from oven and allow the tray to cool to room temperature.

8. Prepare raspberry mousse: whip cream and sugar in electric mixer until stiff peaks form.

9. In the meantime, place the raspberry purée in a separate bowl.

10. Transfer the whipped cream to the bowl of raspberry purée and gently fold together using a rubber spatula.

(continued on next page)

(continued from previous page)

11. After a few folds, before the mixture is fully combined, add in the dissolved gelatin and continue folding until the consistency is smooth.

12. Assemble cake: cut the cake into three 6-inch squares. Cut only the cake, leaving the parchment paper un-cut.

13. Place the cake face down on a work surface and carefully peel off the parchment paper.

14. Place a square of cake on a flat plate or tray and spread with 2 tablespoons of berry sauce. Use ⅓ of the raspberry mousse to pipe on circles (as shown in picture).

15. Top with another square of cake, spread with 2 tablespoons berry sauce. Use another ⅓ of the raspberry mousse to pipe on circles.

16. Place in the freezer for 15 minutes, or in the refrigerator for 40 minutes, so the mousse can set.

17. Remove the cake from the refrigerator or freezer and top with the last square of cake. Use the final ⅓ of raspberry mousse to pipe on circles. Top each circle with a fresh raspberry. Return to freezer.

18. Place the cake in the refrigerator for 30 minutes prior to serving.

19. Store in the refrigerator for up to 24 hours.

Berry Vanilla Bramble Ice Cream Tart

Providing the ultimate balance between sweet and tart, this is an excellent choice for a tart - especially when garnished with assorted fresh and colorful berries.

INGREDIENTS

½ cup cold butter

3 tablespoons powdered sugar

1 egg

1 tablespoon cold water

½ teaspoon salt

1¼ cups flour

Berry Vanilla Bramble Ice Cream (see page 15)

½ cup fresh blueberries

½ cup fresh raspberries

Equipment

One 10-inch tart pan, or four 4-inch individual sized tart pans

Pie weights or dried beans

PREPARATION

1. Place the butter and sugar in a food processor and run for 2 minutes until the mixture is smooth, stopping occasionally to scrape down the sides with a rubber spatula.

2. Stop the food processor and add the egg, water, and salt. Run for another 2 minutes until the mixture is smooth and uniform.

3. Stop the food processor again and add the flour. Run for 1 minute until a ball of dough is formed. Remove the ball from the food processor and cover with cling wrap. Place in the refrigerator for a minimum of 1 hour, or until ready for use.

4. The dough can be kept in the freezer for up to 2 months. To defrost, remove from the freezer and allow it to defrost at room temperature.

5. On a floured work surface, roll out the dough to ⅛ inch thick, then transfer to a tart pan and mold into pan using your fingers. Using a sharp knife, slice off any dough hanging over the side of the tart. If you´re using the 4-inch pans, repeat this with the rest of the tart pans.

(continued on next page)

(continued from previous page)

6. Once the dough is placed in the tart pan, line with aluminum foil. Weight down paper with pie weights or dried beans. Place in a preheated 375°F oven and bake for 20-25 minutes.

7. Remove the tart from the oven, quickly take off the aluminum foil and the weights or beans, and set aside. (You can re-use the foil and beans a number of times.) Place the tart pan on a wire rack to cool for half an hour.

8. Assemble tart: remove the piecrust from the tart pan and fill with scoops of Berry Vanilla Bramble Ice Cream, placed close together, until the entire crust is generously filled with ice cream. Top with the fresh blueberries and raspberries. If you're using 4-inch plates, repeat the process.

9. Serve immediately.

Cakes for Special Occasions

Christmas Cake

•

Raspberry Black Forest Cake

•

Cream Cheese Mousse with Blueberry Jam

•

Chocolate Torte with Strawberry and Vanilla Mousse

•

Almond Torte with Light and Dark Chocolate Mousse

•

Birthday Cake

•

A Grown-Up Birthday Cake

•

Rainbow Torte

Christmas Cake

Serves

8

Not only is this cake very tasty, but it stays fresh for at least 4 days after baking. For a more decadent dessert, serve this cake with a scoop of Candied Fruit Freak Ice Cream (see recipe page 36).

INGREDIENTS

½ cup raisins

½ cup dried cranberries

½ cup walnuts

½ cup dried cherries

¾ cup dark rum

4 eggs

1 cup sugar

1 cup canola oil

1 cup flour + ½ cup flour (to mix with the dried fruit)

2 tablespoons canola oil (to grease the pan)

Equipment

One 10-inch spring form pan

PREPARATION

1. Soak the raisins, cranberries, walnuts, and cherries in rum for at least 1 hour.

2. Beat the eggs in an electric mixer until soft and creamy.

3. Slowly add the sugar until it has all been absorbed into the eggs and stiff peaks form.

4. Slowly, in a thin stream, add the canola oil while continuing to mix. Continue mixing until all the oil has been absorbed and the texture is similar to light mayonnaise.

5. Transfer to a large bowl and add 1 cup flour, while folding with a rubber spatula.

6. Add the other ½ cup of flour to the bowl of soaking dried fruits and stir.

7. Add the fruits to the batter and carefully fold together.

8. Transfer the mixture to the spring form baking pan, lightly greased with canola oil.

9. Place in a 375°F preheated oven for 45 minutes.

10. Remove the cake from the oven and cool on a wire rack until completely cool.

11. Serve fresh or wrap in plastic cling wrap and store in the refrigerator for up to 3 days.

12. Before serving, let the season inspire your decoration - use a seasonal stencil and powdered sugar to create the Santa Claus image as shown.

Raspberry Black Forest Cake

Serves

8

This is an upgraded version of the classic Black Forest Cake, using raspberries instead of cherries.

INGREDIENTS

Torte Dough

4 egg whites

½ cup sugar

4 egg yolks

½ cup flour

¼ cup cocoa

Chocolate Mousse

6 ounces bittersweet chocolate

1 tablespoon butter

1½ cups whipping cream

½ cup sugar

1 teaspoon gelatin powder dissolved in 4 tablespoons boiling water

Syrup

½ cup water

½ cup sugar

1 cup frozen raspberries

PREPARATION

1. Beat the egg whites in an electric mixer until a creamy consistency is achieved.

2. Slowly add half the sugar, while beating, until stiff peaks form. Transfer to a large bowl.

3. Beat the egg yolks and remaining sugar in an electric mixer until the consistency is smooth. Add to the egg whites.

4. Add the flour and cocoa and gently fold into the egg mixture with a rubber spatula until smooth.

5. Pour batter onto the parchment lined baking sheet and spread using a palette knife to achieve an even height.

6. Place baking sheet in 375°F preheated oven and bake for 15 minutes.

7. Remove from oven, place on a wire rack and cool to room temperature.

8. Prepare chocolate mousse: melt chocolate and butter in microwave.

9. Whip cream and sugar in electric mixer until just before stiff peaks form.

(continued on page 120)

(continued from page 118)

Chocolate Ganache Coating

9 ounces bittersweet chocolate

½ cup whipping cream

1 handful raspberries, preferably fresh (for decoration)

Equipment

Baking sheet lined with parchment paper

One 10-inch wide, 2-inch high cake ring

Piping bag with a ¼ inch circular head

10. Place melted chocolate in a separate mixing bowl.

11. Transfer whipped cream into chocolate and gently fold together using a rubber spatula.

12. After a few folds, before the mixture is fully combined, add in the dissolved gelatin and continue folding until the consistency is smooth.

13. Assemble cake: cut 2 circles out of the cake using the 10-inch cake ring as a guide. Cut only the cake, leaving the parchment paper un-cut.

14. Place the cake face down on a work surface and carefully peel off the parchment paper.

15. Set aside the circles of cake for later use.

16. Prepare syrup: in a small saucepan, heat the water and sugar until boiling point.

17. Place the cake ring on a flat plate or tray. Place a circle of cake inside and top with half of the syrup.

18. Top with half the chocolate mousse, straighten slightly with a spoon, scatter on the frozen raspberries, and then top with another circle of cake.

19. Pour remaining syrup onto the cake and top with the remaining mousse.

20. Straighten this top layer of mousse using a palette knife, until it's smooth and attractive.

21. Place in the freezer for at least 2 hours.

22. Prepare ganache: melt chocolate with whipping cream in the microwave.

23. Whisk the mixture with a handheld whisk until the consistency is smooth.

24. Remove the cake from the freezer, place on a wire rack set on a tray, and remove the cake ring. Pour on the chocolate ganache so that it covers the entire cake.

25. Allow the cake to stand for at least half an hour and then return to freezer for another half an hour.

26. Remove the tray from the freezer and scrape the fallen bits of chocolate topping off the tray.

27. Transfer the scraped bits to a piping bag with a ¼ inch circular head.

28. Pipe 8 small circles onto the top of the cake.

29. Place a fresh raspberry onto each circle. Serve immediately or store in the refrigerator for up to 3 days.

Cream Cheese Mousse with Blueberry Jam

Makes

6

This cake is a tasty and refreshing dessert. The classic cheesecake topping of blueberry sauce is used ever so simply by topping with blueberry jam.

INGREDIENTS

Torte Dough

4 egg whites

½ cup sugar

4 egg yolks

½ cup flour

¼ cup cocoa

Cream Cheese Mousse

1 cup whipping cream

½ cup sugar

1 cup cream cheese

½ teaspoon vanilla extract

1 teaspoon gelatin powder dissolved in 4 tablespoons boiling water

Syrup

½ cup water

½ cup sugar

¾ cup blueberry jam

Equipment

Baking sheet lined with parchment paper

Six 3-inch wide, 2-inch high cake rings

PREPARATION

1. Beat the egg whites in an electric mixer until consistency is creamy.

2. Slowly add half the sugar, while beating, until stiff peaks form. Transfer to a large bowl.

3. Beat the egg yolks and remaining sugar in an electric mixer until consistency is smooth. Add to the egg whites.

4. Add the flour and cocoa and gently fold into the egg mixture with a rubber spatula until smooth.

5. Pour batter onto the parchment lined baking sheet and spread using a palette knife to achieve an even height.

6. Place baking sheet in 375°F preheated oven and bake for 15 minutes.

7. Remove from oven and allow the tray to cool until room temperature.

8. Prepare cream cheese mousse: whip cream and sugar in electric mixer until stiff peaks form.

9. In the meantime, place the cheese and vanilla in a separate bowl and mix until cheese is soft.

10. Once the cream is whipped, transfer cream to the bowl of cheese and gently fold together using a rubber spatula.

(continued on page 124)

(continued from page 122)

While this recipe calls for small single serving cakes, it may also be used for a single larger cake.

11. After a few folds, before the mixture is fully combined, add in the dissolved gelatin and continue folding until consistency is smooth.

12. Assemble cakes: cut 6 circles out of the cake using a 3-inch cake ring as a guide. Cut only the cake, leaving the parchment paper un-cut.

13. Place the cake face down on a work surface and carefully peel off the parchment paper.

14. Set aside the circles of cake for later use.

15. Prepare syrup: in a small saucepan, heat the water and sugar until boiling point.

16. Place each cake ring on a flat plate. Place a circle of cake inside and top with syrup.

17. Top each circle with mousse almost to the top of the ring, leaving some room for the blueberry jam.

18. Place all 6 cakes in the freezer for at least 2 hours, but no more than 3 days.

19. Remove cakes from freezer and top with a tablespoon of blueberry jam, straightening with a palette knife.

20. Serve immediately or store in the freezer for up 3 days, or in the refrigerator for up to 2 days.

Chocolate Torte with Strawberry and Vanilla Mousse

Serves

8

A creamy take on strawberry shortcake – except here the strawberry mousse is sandwiched between layers of chocolate cake! Perfect for those who agree that strawberries and chocolate are a heavenly combination.

INGREDIENTS

Torte Dough

4 egg whites

½ cup sugar

4 egg yolks

½ cup flour

¼ cup cocoa

Strawberry Mousse

1½ cups whipping cream

¼ cup sugar

1 cup strawberry purée

1 teaspoon gelatin powder, dissolved in 4 tablespoons boiling water

Vanilla Mousse

1½ cups whipping cream

¼ cup sugar

1 tablespoon pure vanilla extract

1 teaspoon gelatin powder, dissolved in 4 tablespoons boiling water

PREPARATION

1. Beat the egg whites in an electric mixer until consistency is creamy.

2. Slowly add half the sugar, while beating, until stiff peaks form. Transfer to a large bowl.

3. Beat the egg yolks and remaining sugar in an electric mixer until consistency is smooth. Add to the egg whites.

4. Add the flour and the cocoa and gently fold into the egg mixture with a rubber spatula until smooth.

5. Pour batter onto the parchment lined baking sheet and spread using a palette knife to achieve an even height.

6. Place baking sheet in 375°F preheated oven and bake for 15 minutes.

7. Remove from oven and allow the tray to cool until room temperature.

8. Prepare strawberry mousse: whip cream and sugar in electric mixer until stiff peaks form.

9. In the meantime, place the strawberry purée in a separate bowl.

10. Transfer the whipped cream to the bowl of strawberry purée and gently fold together using a rubber spatula.

(continued on next page)

(continued from previous page)

Syrup

½ cup water

½ cup sugar

Equipment

Baking sheet lined with parchment paper

One 10-inch wide, 2-inch high cake ring

11. After a few folds, before the mixture is fully combined, add in the dissolved gelatin and continue folding until the consistency is smooth.

12. Prepare vanilla mousse: whip cream and sugar in electric mixer until stiff peaks form.

13. Add vanilla and gently fold together using a rubber spatula.

14. After a few folds, before the mixture is fully combined, add in the dissolved gelatin and continue folding until the consistency is smooth.

15. Assemble cake: cut 2 circles out of the cake using the 10-inch cake ring as a guide. Cut only the cake, leaving the parchment paper un-cut.

16. Place the cake face down on a work surface and carefully peel off the parchment paper.

17. Set aside the circles of cake for later use.

18. Prepare syrup: in a small saucepan, heat the water and sugar until boiling point.

19. Place the cake ring on a flat plate or tray. Place a circle of cake inside and top with half the syrup.

20. Top with the strawberry mousse, straighten slightly with a spoon, then top with another circle of cake and pour on the remaining syrup.

21. Top with the vanilla mousse and straighten this top layer using a palette knife until smooth and attractive.

22. Place in the freezer for at least 2 hours, but no more than 3 days.

23. Remove cake from freezer 30 minutes prior to serving.

24. Store in the refrigerator for up to 3 days.

Almond Torte with Light and Dark Chocolate Mousse

Serves

8

Attention all chocolate addicts: If chocolate is your thing and you like the delicate crunch of slivered almonds, this is the cake for you.

INGREDIENTS

Torte Dough

4 egg whites

½ cup sugar

4 egg yolks

½ cup flour

¼ cup cocoa

Dark Chocolate Mousse

6 ounces bittersweet chocolate

1 tablespoon butter

1 cup whipping cream

½ cup sugar

1 teaspoon gelatin powder dissolved in 4 tablespoons boiling water

Light Chocolate Mousse

3 ounces bittersweet chocolate

1 tablespoon butter

1 cup whipping cream

½ cup sugar

1 teaspoon gelatin powder dissolved in 4 tablespoons boiling water

PREPARATION

1. Beat the egg whites in an electric mixer until consistency is creamy.

2. Slowly add half the sugar, while beating, until stiff peaks form. Transfer to a large bowl.

3. Beat the egg yolks and remaining sugar in an electric mixer until consistency is smooth. Add to the egg whites.

4. Add the flour and cocoa and gently fold into the egg mixture with a rubber spatula until smooth.

5. Pour batter onto the parchment lined baking sheet and spread using a palette knife to achieve an even height.

6. Place baking sheet in 375°F preheated oven and bake for 15 minutes.

7. Remove from oven and allow the tray to cool until room temperature.

8. Prepare dark chocolate mousse: melt chocolate and butter in microwave.

9. Whip cream and sugar in electric mixer until just before stiff peaks form.

10. Transfer whipped cream into chocolate and gently fold together using a rubber spatula.

(continued on page 130)

(continued from page 128)

Syrup

½ cup water

½ cup sugar

½ cup roasted almonds

Chocolate Ganache Coating

9 ounces bittersweet chocolate

½ cup whipping cream

½ cup slivered almonds (for decoration)

Equipment

Baking sheet lined with parchment paper

One 10-inch wide, 2-inch high cake ring

Piping bag with a ¼ inch circular head

11. After a few folds, before the mixture is fully combined, add in the dissolved gelatin and continue folding until consistency is smooth.

12. Prepare light chocolate mousse: melt chocolate and butter in microwave.

13. Whip cream and sugar in electric mixer until just before stiff peaks form.

14. Transfer whipped cream into chocolate and gently fold together using a rubber spatula.

15. After a few folds, before the mixture is fully combined, add in the dissolved gelatin and continue folding until consistency is smooth.

16. Assemble cake: cut 2 circles out of the cake using the 10-inch cake ring as a guide. Cut only the cake, leaving the parchment paper un-cut.

17. Place the cake face down on a work surface and carefully peel off the parchment paper.

18. Set aside the circles of cake for later use.

19. Prepare syrup: in a small saucepan, heat the water and sugar until boiling point.

20. Place the cake ring on a flat plate or tray. Place a circle of cake inside and top with half the syrup.

21. Top with dark chocolate mousse, straighten slightly with a spoon, sprinkle on the roasted almonds, then top with another circle of cake and pour on the remaining syrup.

22. Top with the light chocolate mousse and straighten this top layer using a palette knife until smooth and attractive.

23. Place in the freezer for at least 2 hours, but no more than 3 days.

24. Prepare ganache: melt chocolate and cream in the microwave.

25. Whisk the mixture with a handheld whisk until texture is smooth and combined.

26. Remove the cake from the freezer and place on a wire rack set on a tray.

27. Remove the cake ring and pour on the chocolate so that it covers the entire cake.

28. Allow the cake to stand for at least half an hour, then return to freezer for another half an hour.

29. Remove the tray from the freezer and scrape the fallen bits of chocolate topping off the tray.

30. Transfer the scraped bits to a piping bag with a ¼ inch circular head.

31. Pipe 8 small circles onto the top of the cake.

32. Place a slice of almond onto each circle.

33. Stick the rest of the almonds all around the sides of the cake.

34. Serve immediately or store in the refrigerator for up to 3 days.

Birthday Cake

My kids are connoisseurs when it comes to the sweets, so I can't get away with just any old birthday cake. On my kid's birthdays I always make this recipe, and all the kids gulp it down in no time flat.

INGREDIENTS

Cake

12 ounces bittersweet chocolate

1 cup butter

10 eggs

2 cup sugar

1 cup flour

Chocolate Ganache Frosting

1 cup whipping cream

¼ cup sugar

9 ounces bittersweet chocolate

Equipment

One 11-inch spring form pan

One 7-inch spring form pan

This recipe can also be prepared as a single layer cake.

PREPARATION

1. Melt the chocolate and butter in a large bowl placed over a pot of boiling water.

2. Beat eggs and sugar in an electric mixer until stiff peaks form.

3. Once the chocolate and butter have melted, remove from heat and fold the flour into the chocolate with a rubber spatula. Fold into the egg mixture.

4. Fill the 11-inch spring form pan ¾ full with batter, and then pour the remaining batter into the 7-inch spring form pan.

5. Place both pans in a 375°F preheated oven for 25 minutes.

6. Once the cakes are ready, remove from oven and allow them to cool on a wire rack for half an hour.

7. Prepare ganache: place cream and sugar in a small saucepan and heat until boiling point.

8. Once the cream comes to a boil, remove from heat and add in chocolate. Whisk until the mixture is smooth and fully combined.

9. Set a wire rack over a tray. Place the larger cake on rack, then place the smaller cake on top of the larger one, exactly in the center.

10. Quickly pour on the chocolate so that the entire cake is evenly covered.

11. Place in the freezer for 3 minutes, then transfer to refrigerator. Store in the refrigerator for up to 3 days.

12. For serving, I chose to decorate this cake with all sorts of colorful things that appeal to children. Use your imagination to create your own perfect birthday cake.

A Grown-Up Birthday Cake

Serves

8

When considering what sort of birthday cake to make for an adult, I decided that a classic cake would be just the thing, made from the best ingredients and decorated simply and elegantly with a ganache frosting.

INGREDIENTS

Cake

10 ounces bittersweet chocolate

¾ cup butter

6 eggs

1 cup sugar

1 tablespoon amaretto

½ cup flour

Chocolate Ganache Frosting

½ cup whipping cream

2 tablespoons sugar

5 ounces bittersweet chocolate

Equipment

One 10-inch spring form pan

PREPARATION

1. Melt the chocolate and butter in a large bowl placed over a pot of boiling water.

2. Beat eggs and sugar in an electric mixer until stiff peaks form.

3. Once the chocolate and butter have melted, remove from heat and mix in the amaretto, using a rubber spatula.

4. Fold the flour into the chocolate with a rubber spatula, and then fold in the egg mixture.

5. Pour the batter into baking pan.

6. Place pan in a 375°F preheated oven for 25 minutes.

7. Once the cake is ready, remove from oven and allow it to cool on a wire rack for half a hour.

8. Prepare ganache: place cream and sugar in a small saucepan and heat until boiling point.

9. Once the cream comes to a boil, remove from heat and add in chocolate. Whisk until the mixture is smooth and fully combined.

10. Set a wire rack over a tray. Place cake on rack and quickly pour on the chocolate so that it covers the entire cake evenly.

11. Place in the freezer for 3 minutes, then transfer to refrigerator. Store in the refrigerator for up to 3 days.

12. For serving, I chose to adorn this cake with green and blue sugar flowers and elegant candles. Decorate the cake anyway you like, including piping a birthday greeting onto the face of the cake.

Rainbow Torte

*This four-tiered torte features four different tasty mousses.
It´s as impressive to look at as it is to eat.*

INGREDIENTS

Torte Dough

4 egg whites

½ cup sugar

4 egg yolks

½ cup flour

¼ cup cocoa

Strawberry Mousse

1 cup cream

½ cup sugar

½ cup strawberry purée

1 teaspoon gelatin powder dissolved in
4 tablespoons boiling water

Syrup

½ cup water

½ cup sugar

Pistachio Mousse

1 cup whipping cream

½ cup sugar

2 tablespoons natural pistachio paste

1 teaspoon gelatin powder dissolved in
4 tablespoons boiling water

PREPARATION

1. Beat the egg whites in an electric mixer until the consistency is creamy.

2. Slowly add half the sugar, while beating, until stiff peaks form. Transfer to a large bowl.

3. Beat the egg yolks and remaining sugar in an electric mixer until a smooth consistency is achieved, and add to the egg whites.

4. Add the flour and cocoa, and gently fold into the egg mixture with a rubber spatula until smooth.

5. Pour batter onto the parchment lined baking sheet and spread using a palette knife to achieve an even height.

6. Place baking sheet in a 375°F preheated oven and bake for 15 minutes.

7. Remove from oven, place on wire rack and cool to room temperature.

8. Prepare strawberry mousse: whip cream and sugar in electric mixer until stiff peaks form.

9. In the meantime, place the strawberry purée in a separate bowl.

10. Transfer the whipped cream to the bowl of strawberry purée and gently fold together using a rubber spatula.

(continued on page 138)

(continued from page 136)

Blueberry Mousse

1 cup whipping cream

½ cup sugar

½ cup blueberry purée

1 teaspoon gelatin powder dissolved in 4 tablespoons boiling water

Mango Mousse

1 cup whipping cream

½ cup sugar

½ cup ripe mango purée

1 teaspoon gelatin powder dissolved in 4 tablespoons boiling water

Thin slices of fresh mango (for decoration)

Equipment

Baking sheet lined with parchment paper

One 7-inch cake ring

11. After a few folds, before the mixture is fully combined, add in the dissolved gelatin and then continue folding until the mixture has a smooth consistency.

12. Assemble cake: cut 3 circles out of the cake using the 7-inch cake ring as a guide. Cut only the cake, leaving the parchment paper un-cut.

13. Place the cake face down on a work surface and carefully peel off the parchment paper.

14. Set aside the circles of cake for later use.

15. Prepare syrup: in a small saucepan, heat the water and sugar until boiling point.

16. Place the cake ring on a flat plate or tray. Place a circle of cake inside and top with ⅓ of the syrup.

17. Top with the strawberry mousse, straighten slightly with a spoon and then top with another circle of cake.

18. Pour another ⅓ of the syrup onto the cake.

19. Place in the freezer.

20. Prepare pistachio mousse: whip cream and sugar in electric mixer until stiff peaks form.

21. In the meantime, place the pistachio paste in a separate bowl.

22. Transfer the whipped cream to the bowl of pistachio paste and gently fold together using a rubber spatula.

23. After a few folds, before the mixture is fully combined, add in the dissolved gelatin and continue folding until the mixture has a smooth consistency.

24. Take the cake out of the freezer and pour on the pistachio mousse.

25. Straighten with a spoon and top with the last circle of cake.

26. Pour on the remaining syrup and return to the freezer.

27. Prepare blueberry mousse: whip cream and sugar in electric mixer until stiff peaks form.

28. In the meantime, place the blueberry purée in a separate bowl.

29. Transfer the whipped cream to the bowl of blueberry purée and gently fold together using a rubber spatula.

30. After a few folds, before the mixture is fully combined, add in the dissolved gelatin and continue folding until a smooth consistent mixture is achieved.

31. Take the cake out of the freezer, pour on the blueberry mousse, straighten with a spoon and return to the freezer.

32. Prepare mango mousse: whip cream and sugar in electric mixer until stiff peaks form.

33. In the meantime, place the mango purée in a separate bowl.

34. Transfer the whipped cream to the bowl of mango purée and gently fold together using a rubber spatula.

35. After a few folds, before the mixture is fully combined, add in the dissolved gelatin and continue folding until the mixture has a smooth consistency.

36. Take the cake out of the freezer and pour on the mango mousse.

37. Straighten with a palette knife so that this top layer of mousse is perfectly smooth and attractive.

38. Return to the freezer for at least 2 hours. Defrost 30-40 minutes before serving. Remove cake ring and decorate the top with fresh mango. I also chose to add raspberries for added color and elegance – use any fresh fruit you like. The cake can be kept in the refrigerator for up to 2 days.

Tools and Ingredients

TOOLS

Cake Ring

Cake rings are needed to help mousse cakes to keep their shape until serving time. If you haven't got one, you can use a round spring form pan of the same size instead.

Candy Thermometer

This is an excellent tool for gauging the heat of liquids as they cook. In ice cream making, this is an essential tool to ensure that the egg yolk mixtures (or custards) have reached, but not surpassed, the desired temperature.

Ice Cream Maker

There are 3 main types of ice cream makers:

No Cooler: The first, simplest ice cream maker doesn't have a cooler. In this case, you must chill the ice cream mixture almost to the point of freezing, and then place the entire ice cream maker in the freezer where it will mix and freeze the ice cream.

With Cooler: The second ice cream maker has a cooler and a double walled pot in which you place the mixture. The ice cream maker chills while it mixes so that as the ice cream is cooling, air is added. This results in ice cream of a light consistency.

Low Volume Industrial: The third ice cream maker is a low volume industrial machine. This ice cream maker works in a similar way to the previous two, but the cooling output is different. This ice cream maker turns the liquid mixture into ice cream in a matter of minutes and can absorb a lot of air, creating an especially light ice cream.

Electric Mixer

Ideal for creaming butter and sugar for cake batters.

Palette Knife

This tool is handy not only for icing cakes, but also for smoothing out ice cream or mousse cakes before they set in the freezer.

Parchment Paper

This is needed to line baking sheets. It prevents cake from sticking and makes removal from pan or sheet much easier.

Piping/Pastry Bag with Tip

Some of the recipes in this book call for the use of a piping bag with a round tip of varying sizes. If you don't have one, you can easily make a homemade substitute by wrapping parchment paper into a cone shape and filling it with batter, mousse, ganache or frosting. Alternately, you can place the filling in a resealable plastic bag and snip off one of the bottom corners.

Saucepan

The heavier the pan bottom, the better, especially when caramelizing nuts.

Spring Form Pan

Specified in most of the ice cream cake recipes, these pans are ideal when making ice cream cakes because they facilitate easy removal from the ring.

INGREDIENTS

Cream

Always use fresh cream with the highest fat content available. It's often called whipping cream or double cream.

Eggs

Always use large eggs and the freshest available.

Milk

Always use fresh milk, at least 3% fat.

Vanilla

Use pure liquid vanilla extract or a vanilla bean. As a rule of thumb, 1 teaspoon vanilla extract is equivalent to half a vanilla bean.

Metric Equivalents

The recipes that appear in this cookbook use the standard United States method for measuring liquid and dry or solid ingredients (teaspoons, tablespoons, and cups). The information on this chart is provided to help cooks outside the U.S. successfully use these recipes. All equivalents are approximate.

METRIC EQUIVALENTS FOR DIFFERENT TYPES OF INGREDIENTS

A standard cup measure of a dry or solid ingredient will vary in weight depending on the type of ingredient. A standard cup of liquid is the same volume for any type of liquid. Use the following chart when converting standard cup measures to grams (weight) or milliliters (volume).

Standard Cup	Fine Powder (ex. flour)	Grain (ex. rice)	Granular (ex. sugar)	Liquid Solids (ex. butter)	liquid (ex. milk)
1	140 g	150 g	190 g	200 g	240 ml
¾	105 g	113 g	143 g	150 g	180 ml
⅔	93 g	100 g	125 g	133 g	160 ml
½	70 g	75 g	95 g	100 g	120 ml
⅓	47 g	50 g	63 g	67 g	80 ml
¼	35 g	38 g	48 g	50 g	60 ml
⅛	18 g	19 g	24 g	25 g	30 ml

USEFUL EQUIVALENTS FOR DRY INGREDIENTS BY WEIGHT

(To convert ounces to grams, multiply the number of ounces by 30.)

1 oz	=	¹⁄₁₆ lb	=	30 g
4 oz	=	¼ lb	=	120 g
8 oz	=	½ lb	=	240 g
12 oz	=	¾ lb	=	360 g
16 oz	=	1 lb	=	480 g

USEFUL EQUIVALENTS FOR LENGTH

(To convert inches to centimeters, multiply the number of inches by 2.5.)

1 in			=	2.5 cm		
6 in	=	½ ft	=	15 cm		
12 in	=	1 ft	=	30 cm		
36 in	=	3 ft	=	1 yd	=	90 cm
40 in			=	100 cm	=	1 m

USEFUL EQUIVALENTS FOR DRY INGREDIENTS BY WEIGHT

¼ tsp					=	1 ml				
½ tsp					=	2 ml				
1 tsp					=	5 ml				
3 tsp	=	1 tbls			½ fl oz =	15 ml				
		2 tbls	=	⅛ cup =	1 fl oz =	30 ml				
		4 tbls	=	¼ cup =	2 fl oz =	60 ml				
		5 ⅓ tbls	=	⅓ cup =	3 fl oz =	80 ml				
		8 tbls	=	½ cup =	4 fl oz =	120 ml				
		10 ⅔ tbls	=	⅔ cup =	5 fl oz =	160 ml				
		12 tbls	=	¾ cup =	6 fl oz =	180 ml				
		16 tbls	=	1 cup =	8 fl oz =	240 ml				
		1 pt	=	2 cups =	16 fl oz =	480 ml				
		1 qt	=	4 cups =	32 fl oz =	960 ml				
				=	33 fl oz =	1000 ml	= 1 liter			

USEFUL EQUIVALENTS FOR
COOKING/OVEN TEMPERATURES

	Fahrenheit	Celsius	Gas Mark
Freeze Water	32° F	0° C	
Room Temperature	68° F	20° C	
Boil Water	212° F	100° C	
Bake	325° F	160° C	3
	350° F	180° C	4
	375° F	190° C	5
	400° F	200° C	6
	425° F	220° C	7
	450° F	230° C	8
Broil			Grill

Index

A

A Grown-Up Birthday Cake, 115, 135
Almonds, 67, 128, 130, 131
  Almond Torte with Light and Dark Chocolate
    Mousse, 128
  Apricot Almond Indulgence Sorbet, 57, 67
  Grilled Peaches with Candied Almond Craze Ice
    Cream and Amaretto Sauce, 73
Amaretto, 22, 67, 81, 105, 106, 135
Apples, 60
  Granny Green Apple Sorbet, 57, 60
Apricot, 14, 67, 81
  Apricot Almond Indulgence Sorbet, 57, 67
  Apricot and Cherry Ice Cream Cake, 93, 99
  Apricot Ape Ice Cream, 7, 14, 99, 100

B

Baked Pears with Vanilla Ice Cream and Caramel, 73
Bananas, 74, 77
  Banana Split, 73, 74
Belgian Waffle, 73, 77
Berries, 15, 53, 78, 85, 111
  Berry Sauce, 39, 53, 73, 85, 91
  Berry Vanilla Bramble Ice Cream, 7, 15, 93,
    111, 112
  Berry Vanilla Bramble Ice Cream Tart, 111
Black Forest Cherry Sorbet, 57, 64, 99
Blueberry, 7, 16, 71, 85, 109, 111, 112, 115, 122,
  124, 136, 138, 139
  Blue-berriness Sorbet, 57, 71
  Blueberry Vanilla Nights Ice Cream, 7, 16
  Cream Cheese Mousse with Blueberry Jam,
    115, 122
  Rainbow Torte, 115, 136
Brandy, 36, 63
  Orange Brandy Sorbet, 63
Brownie, 8, 35, 73, 89
  Brownie Sundae with Vanilla Ice Cream and Hot
    Chocolate Sauce, 73
Butterscotch Sauce, 39, 55

C

Cachaça, 29, 57, 68
  Cachaça Passion Sorbet, 68
  Tropical Treat Ice Cream, 7, 29
Candied Fruit Freak Ice Cream, 8, 36
Candied Pecan and Peanut Butter Explosion Cream
  Pie, 93
Candied Pecan and Peanut Butter Explosion Ice
  Cream, 7, 30, 103
Cantaloupe Cool Sorbet, 57, 64
Caramel, 39, 43, 73, 81, 82, 91, 93, 97, 98
  Baked Pears with Caramel and Vanilla Ice
    Cream, 82
  Caramel and Crumble Vanilla Ice Cream Cake,
    93, 97
  Caramel Sauce, 39, 43
Cherries, 64, 116, 118
  Apricot and Cherry Ice Cream Cake, 99
  Black Forest Cherry Sorbet, 57, 64, 99
Cherry liqueur, 64, 71

Chocolate

A Grown-Up Birthday Cake, 115, 135
Birthday Cake, 115, 133
Brownie, 8, 35, 73, 89
Chocolate Brownie Bump Ice Cream, 8, 35
Chocolate Fudge Ice Cream Tart, 93, 95
Chocolate Fudge Thud Ice Cream, 7, 33, 95
Chocolate Log with Vanilla Ice Cream and
  Berries, 73, 78
Chocolate Torte with Raspberry Mousse, 93, 109
Chocolate Torte with Strawberry and Vanilla
  Mousse, 115
Ganache, 118, 120, 130, 131, 133, 135, 141
Coconut, 10, 54
Coffee, 50, 55, 105, 106
  Butterscotch Sauce, 39, 55
  Coffee-Biscuit Break Ice Cream, 7, 25
  Rich Coffee Sauce, 39, 50
Coffee liqueur, 50
Cranberries, 116
  Christmas Cake, 115, 116
Cream cheese, 122, 124
  Cream Cheese Mousse with Blueberry Jam,
    115, 122

D

Donuts filled with Ice Cream and Berry Sauce, 73
Dried fruit, 116

E

Egg-less Vanilla Ice Cream, 7
Espresso, 25, 55, 105, 106

F

French Vanilla Ice Cream, 15, 16, 20, 22, 23, 26, 29
Frozen Tiramisu, 93, 105
Fudge, 7, 33, 39, 45, 46, 93, 95
  Chocolate Fudge Ice Cream Tart, 93, 95
  Chocolate Fudge Thud Ice Cream, 7, 33, 95
  Hot Chocolate Fudge, 45
  Praline Fudge, 46
  Peanut Butter Fudge, 46

G

Granny Green Apple Sorbet, 57, 60
Grilled Peaches with Candied Almond Craze Ice
  Cream and Amaretto Sauce, 73

H

Hazelnut Praline Paste, 46
Hot Chocolate Fudge, 45

I

Ice-Cream Sandwiches, 73, 86
Italian Vanilla Ice Cream, 14, 19, 25, 30, 33, 35

J

Jack Daniels, 23
Jackie D. Chocolate Ice Cream, 7, 23

L

Lemon
  Lemon Zest, 51
  Rich Lemon Sauce, 39, 51
Light Chocolate Sauce, 39, 42
Lime Juice, 63
  Tequila Lime Shot Sorbet, 57, 63
Lychee, 29
  Tropical Treat Ice Cream, 7, 29

M

Mango, 29, 67, 138, 139
  Mango Madness Sorbet, 57, 67, 91
  Mango Popsicle, 73, 91
  Rainbow Torte, 115, 136
  Tropical Treat Ice Cream, 7, 29
Marzipan, 7, 22, 81
  Mediterranean Marzipan Ice Cream, 7, 22, 81

O

Orange Brandy Sorbet, 57, 63
Orange Juice, 48, 63
  Orange Pineapple Sauce, 39, 48
  Orange Brandy Sorbet, 57, 63

P

Passion Fruit, 26, 68
  Pure Passion Ice Cream, 7, 26
Pavlova, 73, 85
Peaches, 60
  Grilled Peaches with Candied Almond Craze Ice
    Cream and Amaretto Sauce, 73
  White Peachy Keen Sorbet, 57, 60
Peanut Butter, 7, 30, 32, 39, 46, 47, 93, 103, 104
  Candied Pecan and Peanut Butter Explosion
    Cream Pie, 93
  Candied Pecan and Peanut Butter Explosion Ice
    Cream, 7, 30, 103
Pears, 73, 82
  Baked Pears with Vanilla Ice Cream and Caramel,
    73
  Pretty Pear Sorbet, 59
Pecan, 7, 30, 32, 93, 103
  Candied Pecan and Peanut Butter Explosion
    Cream Pie, 93
  Candied Pecan and Peanut Butter Explosion Ice
    Cream, 7, 30, 103
Pineapple, 29, 48, 71
  Orange Pineapple Sauce, 39, 48
  Pineapple Rum Ball Sorbet, 57, 71
  Tropical Treat Ice Cream, 7, 29
Pistachio, 7, 20, 136
  Pleasing Pistachio Ice Cream, 7, 20
Pomegranate, 47, 68
  Pomegranate Punch Sorbet, 57, 68
Pure Passion Ice Cream, 7, 26

R

Rainbow Torte, 115, 136

Raspberries, 85, 109, 110, 111, 112, 118, 120
  Raspberry Black Forest Cake, 115, 118
  Chocolate Torte with Raspberry Mousse, 93, 109
Rose Scented Pomegranate Sauce, 39, 47
Rose water extract, 47
Rum, 29, 71, 116
  Pineapple Rum Ball Sorbet, 57, 71
  Tropical Treat Ice Cream, 7, 29

S

Schnapps, 60, 64
  Cantaloupe Cool Sorbet, 57, 64
  White Peachy Keen Sorbet, 57, 60
Strawberry, 19, 77, 125, 126, 136, 138, 139
  Strawberry-licious Vanilla Ice Cream, 19
  Rainbow Torte, 115, 136
Sundae, 74, 89
  Brownie Sundae with Vanilla Ice Cream and Hot
    Chocolate Sauce, 73

T

Tequila, 63
  Tequila Lime Shot Sorbet, 57, 63
Triple Sec, 68
  Pomegranate Punch Sorbet, 57, 68
Tropical Treat Ice Cream, 7, 29

V

Vanilla
  Berry Vanilla Bramble Ice Cream, 7, 15, 93,
    111, 112
  Baked Pears with Caramel and Vanilla Ice
    Cream, 82
  Blueberry Vanilla Nights Ice Cream, 7, 16
  Brownie Sundae with Vanilla Ice Cream and Hot
    Chocolate Sauce, 73
  Caramel and Crumble Vanilla Ice Cream Cake,
    93, 97
  Chocolate Log with Vanilla Ice Cream and
    Berries, 78
  Donuts filled with Ice Cream and Berry Sauce, 73
  Egg-less Vanilla Ice Cream, 7
  French Vanilla Ice Cream, 15, 16, 20, 22, 23,
    26, 29
  Italian Vanilla Ice Cream, 14, 19, 25, 30, 33, 35
  Really Vanilla Sauce, 40
  Vanilla Pavlova with Vanilla Ice Cream and Berry
    Sauce, 73, 85

W

Waffle, 77
  Belgian Waffle, 73, 77
Walnuts, 109, 116
  Christmas Cake, 115, 116
  Raspberry Charlotte, 93, 109
White Peachy Keen Sorbet, 57, 60